Golf in My Gallowses

Golf in My Gallowses

Angus MacVicar

partnered by Jock MacVicar

Confessions of a Fairway Fanatic

Hutchinson
London Melbourne Sydney Auckland Johannesburg

Hutchinson & Co. (Publishers) Ltd
An imprint of the Hutchinson Publishing Group
17-21 Conway Street, London W1P 6JD

Hutchinson Group (Australia) Pty Ltd
30–32 Cremorne Street, Richmond South, Victoria 3121
PO Box 151, Broadway, New South Wales 2007

Hutchinson Group (NZ) Ltd
32–34 View Road, PO Box 40-086, Glenfield, Auckland 10

Hutchinson Group (SA) Pty Ltd
PO Box 337, Bergvlei 2012, South Africa

First published 1983
© Angus MacVicar 1983

Set in Linotron Times by
Book Economy Services, Burgess Hill, Sussex

Printed in Great Britain by The Anchor Press Ltd
and bound by Wm Brendon & Son Ltd,
both of Tiptree, Essex

British Library Cataloguing in Publication Data

MacVicar, Angus
    Golf in my gallowses.
    1. Golf – Anecdotes, facetiae, satire, etc
    I. Title   II. MacVicar, Jock
    796.352   GV967

ISBN 0 09 154160 3

Gallowses: According to *Chambers Twentieth Century Dictionary* a word 'used colloquially, especially in Scotland, for a pair of braces (in America, suspenders) for supporting the trousers'.

To Lavinia Derwent
who knows very little about
golf but everything about
writing good books

Card for the Course

Illustrations

Acknowledgements

For permission to reproduce photographs our grateful thanks are due especially to the *Daily Express*; also to David Hamilton (author of *The Good Golf Guide to Scotland*), to Jack Crombie of the *Scotsman*, Kenneth MacVicar, Margaret Cameron, Gordon Hunter, Arthur Gillies and the Dunaverty Golf Club.

For certain facts and figures which buttress our flights of fancy we are greatly indebted to *The Golfers' Handbook* and to *The Game With The Hole In It* by Peter Dobereiner (Faber & Faber, 1970); also to *The Golfers* (Collins, 1982) compiled from writings by members of the Association of Golf Writers, to *Golf From Two Sides* by Roger and Joyce Wethered (Longmans, Green & Co, 1922), *Bobby Locke on Golf* (Country Life, 1953), *Love That Golf* by Don Herold (The World's Work, 1913) and *The Golfer Who Laughed* by Phil Tressider (Stanley Paul, 1982).

Finally, we acknowledge that no character in this book is fictitious and that every story we tell contains the truth as we see it. (Duck for cover, Jock!)

A.M.
A.J.M.

1. A Hint of Paradise

Golf is a game in which you are alone with your Creator.

The course may be crowded with opponents, caddies, spectators and, in the case of Dunaverty, my home course, also with sheep, cattle and dive-bombing terns; but, as you play successive shots, each one consists of a struggle not so much with an adversary as with the swing designed for you by the Almighty. And the Almighty, you suspect, has had a lot of fun creating yours.

There is no meaner opponent than yourself. You loathe the craven elements in your character which cause you to stab at pitches, using too much right hand, and yip short putts past the hole with all the finesse of a woodpecker with *delirium tremens*. Living creatures around you, including cud-chewing cows staring impassively from behind electric fences, may find your antics interesting and even amusing; but you are aware of only one thing: the nobility inherent in your character is receiving yet more body-blows from the evil genius which exists alongside it. Your sour opinion of yourself and your golf overheats to the point of explosion, when clubs and turf are liable to erupt from your presence like jets of steam from a boiler.

But of course, being a faithful golfer and therefore accustomed to enduring torture, on most occasions you will refrain from violence and present a face of stoicism to the world, even offering your neighbours a crooked smile. In the dark caverns of your ego, however, the pain will persist. Faced with accumulating evidence of your weakness and ineptitude, you reach the sad conclusion that your next round may prove an even more difficult challenge to the Almighty's arrangements.

And yet, because you are a faithful golfer, you will continue to have faith in His compassion. If you cling to courage and remain unflagging in resolution, may He not relent and fashion for you a swing that even Sam Snead might envy? Mentally you will rant against the evil within yourself, perhaps, if you are a scholar, using words from Shakespeare: 'Away, you scullion! you rampallion! you fustilarian! I'll tackle your catastrophe!'

Then one day (strangely enough, it is often a day when you are feeling unwell and the prospect, like that of Rabbie Burns, is decidedly 'drear') the Almighty raises a benign finger. Your swing becomes smooth and unhurried, causing your timing to resemble that of Tom Watson and your putts to purr smoothly towards the hole as unerringly as did those of Bobby Locke.

One of the best medal rounds I ever played at Dunaverty was a 66 less 7, 59, compiled during a bout of diarrhoea, when my sole worry concerned the location of the next clump of whins and finicky details of the golf swing were far from my thoughts. Only when I returned home, and an arrowroot pudding with hot milk brought peace to my bowels, did the full glory of that round burgeon in my consciousness. The fact that I had won the competition was irrelevant. The joy came from the knowledge that at last the Almighty had come down on my side with the gift of golf's great secret.

You may raise admiring eyebrows at that 66. Here, you may imagine, is a writer with the golfing skills of a Panton or a Gallacher. I have to confess, however, that Dunaverty's eighteen holes add up to a length of only 4597 yards and that its standard scratch score is 63.

On those ecstatic occasions, when revelation comes, you give thanks to your Creator not only for giving you life but also for giving you life as a golfer. In spite of scudding hail showers, the weather, as far as you are concerned, is passing fair. The views around the course are incredibly beautiful, especially that of the bold bluff of the Mull of Kintyre and the blue hills of Antrim across the North Channel – the view, in fact, from the 11th green where you holed a chip for an eagle 2. Your fellow members are all decent chaps, despite their continual moans about cuppy lies and missed putts, and you can perceive good even in the second oldest member whose putter has wrought evil against you so many times. The caddies and the cattle are endurable. The whisky is wonderfully fragrant. And you fall in love with your wife all over again. Indeed, you are inclined to quote, for the benefit of anyone who will listen, what may be a mystic reference to golf in William Blake's *Jerusalem*:

> I give you the end of a golden string;
> Only wind it into a ball.
> It will lead you to heaven's gate
> Built in Jerusalem's wall.

Is there a hint here as to why so many of us love the game and remain faithful to it despite frequent travail?

MEMO

Acquiring a new set of clubs is rather like getting married. The honeymoon is wonderful but how things go after that depends on whether the courtship has properly tested the true compatibility of the partners. I strongly recommend pre-marital golf to the swain contemplating taking unto himself a set of clubs.

Peter Dobereiner

2. The Beginning of Wisdom

Unbelievers often ask: 'Why do otherwise apparently sensible individuals take up golf?'

One reason is that to some it appears to be an easy game: a game, moreover, generally played in pleasant places and with pleasant companions. Perhaps they have read A.A. Milne's pronouncement that it is 'the best of all games at which to be bad'. Or Bernard Darwin's words concerning the joy of practising even without a partner:

I think not only of quiet corners on many courses, but of many fields where the grass was so long that almost every stroke involved a search. I think of a mountain top in Wales and a plain in Macedonia, of innumerable floors on which I have tried to hit table legs. I recall wind and rain and mud and the shades of evening falling, so that the lights came twinkling out in the houses around the links, and the ball's destiny was a matter of mere conjecture. Remembering all these things, I can say that I may have been an unprofitable practiser, but that at any rate I have been a happy one.

So the gentle reader decides that, like Darwin (who could sound, on his day, like St Paul in one of his Epistles), he will attempt to achieve happiness by playing golf. And he will. Without a doubt, if he perseveres, he will achieve great happiness. But only on certain occasions and at a price.

At the beginning, as a novice, he sees a ball before him. It is not moving, as it does, for example, in shinty or hockey or cricket. He can take all the time in the world to strike it. What could be more simple? Under the eye of a professional or a friend who plays golf, he executes a few practice swings. He smiles with confidence and anticipation and steps forward to the ball. He swipes. He misses it by inches, or even by several feet. He looks up, bewildered, then down again at the ball, still sitting there, inert. The day remains beautiful, with only the sough of the sea and the trill of a lark in the clear air to break the daunting silence.

This is the moment for which the professional or the friend has been waiting. Will the pupil flinch, shrug, throw down his 7-iron and declare that golf is not for him? Or will he steel his nerve and attack the ball again?

The novice decides to attack the ball again. He swings at it. He misses again. A light of anger kindles in his eye. His grim features express a thought: 'You stationary, silent, sneering, *bloody* ball, you're not going to beat me!'

He swings and misses again.

Pride and confidence – and even anger – begin to desert him. He turns to his companions, with a wordless plea for help.

'Slow back,' he is told. 'Left arm straight. Pivot smoothly. Keep your eye on the back of the ball. In to out. Follow through.' (If in Scotland he will be told, more tersely: 'Left airm straucht. Sweevel canny an' keep yer e'e on the erse o' the ba'.')

He tries again, slow back, left arm straight, easy pivot, eyes fixed on the ball, in to out, full follow-through. With a sound like the click of a closing knife-blade the ball flies up from the turf. It soars into a sunlit sky, straight towards the yellow practice flag. In the novice's hands there is a tingle of sensuous delight, in his heart a beat of glory.

His companion smiles – a smile which contains a hint of sympathy, because he knows that in the past few moments he has helped to deliver a special creature: a creature who, though still counted a member of the human race, has been infected with the virulent golf bug and who, from now on, will hack his way through life, seeking shots of utter perfection and enduring misery in varying degrees in the long intervals between them. On the other hand, he is happy for his pupil who, as a faithful golfer, will count such misery as naught when the perfect shots do occur.

> One moment may with bliss repay
> Unnumbered hours of pain.

There is no difference between the degrees of misery and joy experienced by an eighteen-handicapper and a tournament-hardened professional. When Jack Nicklaus sank a putt on the 18th green at St Andrews to beat Doug Sanders in a play-off for the Open Championship in 1970, that otherwise phlegmatic and self-contained golfer threw his putter high in the air in a gesture of sheer joy. As the putter came down it missed Sanders's head by inches and Jack's delight was transmuted at once into voluble apology. But even in his misery Sanders understood. 'Okay, Jack,' he said, quietly. He had lost a once in a lifetime chance of glory – and financial security – but he was still a faithful golfer.

And when Tony Jacklin won the Sun Alliance PGA Championship at Hillside in 1982, after many years without a major win to his credit, he reacted in exactly the same way as a long handicapper does in winning a monthly medal. He did his best to appear modest and sporting; but several times during the post-competition interviews he broke off with a clenching of triumphant fists and an excited muttering: 'I can't believe it! I can't believe it!'

For all his fame and fortune I recognized in Tony a fellow golfer, with the same feelings of misery and joy that beset us all.

There is no doubt that golf can be a valuable aid to success in business. And herein lies another reason for taking up golf. High-powered executives, during their training, are often advised to become acquainted with the game, because nowadays many lucrative deals are negotiated on the course and afterwards clinched in a haze of good fellowship in the clubhouse bar.

All my life I have enjoyed rounds of golf with publishers and editors and have taken care, with a contract in the offing, to arrange that they beat me, albeit narrowly.

This purpose is not as easily achieved as the non-addict may imagine. Publishers and editors, I have found, are seldom expert golfers. They are so accustomed to being in command of their jobs that they believe they are also, by divine right, in command of their golf swing, and they fail, therefore, to practise it with any sense of dedication. When playing against them I am aware of superiority as far as swing practice is concerned. The result is that sometimes I perform far better than I intend to do and, in a close finish, have to resort to dumping approach shots into water hazards and, as a last gambit, to calling penalties on myself for touching and moving balls during the address.

You may argue that this reveals me as a less than faithful golfer, especially in the eyes of those like Bobby Locke, who insists that he has always played to win. But Bobby was – and is – a professional golfer. I am a professional writer, with wolves continually howling at my door, and editors and publishers, with access to substantial bank accounts, are my only defence against them. In order to enjoy golf as an amateur I must earn something to live on during the intervals between games.

An editor came to see me once to discuss a serial story. Before settling the details – and the price – we played over Dunaverty, and I hoped he would acquit himself so well that as we shared drams in the bar afterwards the price might climb high on the ladder of his euphoria.

In the course of the round the weather deteriorated. A gale sprang up. As each gust roared down the valley of the Con I noticed my opponent clutching his thatch of vivid red, and the awful realization came to me that he was wearing a wig. Along the exposed 15th fairway he executed a 3-iron shot. At the finish of his follow-through he posed like a model in *Golf Monthly* to admire and savour it. At that moment his wig flapped and shimmied, flapped and shimmied, then flew up and away, along the wind.

With a feeling of horror I saw that he was as bald as Kojak and that his naked head glowed pink. I averted my eyes, not wishing to add to his embarrassment. As I did so I caught sight of his wig in the near distance, blooming like a great red flower on a clump of whins by the riverside. This gave me an excuse for salutary action. I rushed to retrieve it, aware of sobbing sounds behind me. Was he actually crying? What chance had any writer with an editor who had been caught not only hairless but also shedding tears of shame?

I brought the wig to him. Raising lowered eyes, I found that far from being in need of sympathy he was sobbing with laughter. 'I'll put the bloody thing in my bag till we get to the clubhouse,' he said. 'It happens often in a high wind. Did you see that 3-iron of mine? Beside the pin, old boy!'

I trembled with relief and gratitude. Indeed, I was so unnerved that I struck no other shot worth mentioning, and my editor won the game at the 17th.

It did occur to me that, in fact, he might be as faithful a golfer as I was: even the embarrasment of losing his wig had been overwhelmed by his joy in having played a near-perfect iron shot. And I was beset by another niggling suspicion. Might he not have stage-managed the whole incident to put me off my game? In the circumstances, however, I adopted a Christian attitude and put unworthy thoughts aside. The serial was safe, and after the third double in the bar – and following a long discussion concerning the exquisite precision of his 3-iron at the 15th – he mentioned a price for it which, from my point of view, was satisfactory.

There is yet another reason why some people take up golf. Doctors prescribe it, for health reasons: the health of the brain as well as that of the body. In saying this, however, I keep in mind the words of a well-known Harley Street psychiatrist – words which I cannot guarantee were spoken in jest: 'When a patient comes to me suffering from severe mental strain, my first questions is, "Do you play golf?" If the answer is "No", I advise him to take some lessons. If the answer is "Yes", I tell him to give it up at once.'

In my own case – though I took up the game more than sixty years ago, at an age when health was the least of my worries – I had a feeling that if I missed my regular four-ball I should be hard put to it to write another word. Three hours on the course, battling in the open air with an entirely different set of problems from those which confront me at a stuffy desk, tend to recharge my creative batteries as nothing else can. For me golf is truly re-creation, and I am liable to become boring in my efforts to point this out to those of my young friends upon whom the stresses and strains of modern life appear to be pressing too hard. And it is significant that in spite of what my friend in Harley Street infers, I know of no regular golfer who has experienced a nervous breakdown.

At times, on the course, you may observe players who exhibit suspicious symptoms. (I exhibit them myself, constantly.) Having duffed a short chip, they scream and shout and raise tense arms towards the sky. As their putt for the match misses the hole they collapse on all fours like enraged gorillas, beating the turf with clenched fists. Imprecations are uttered with such teeth-crunching vigour that a frothing at the mouth seems possible. But in the world of golf occurrences like these are normal and no indication at all of mental instability. Afterwards, when off the course, the same individuals will be gentle and loving with their wives and children and extremely kind to the old and frail. The only psychiatrists they are liable to consult will be their local professionals.

In the face of so much dramatic evidence to the contrary, it may appear to laymen incredible that golf should offer therapy to people under stress in their daily work. But it does. I can assure them it does. Perhaps because it involves an entirely different set of brain cells. Perhaps because letting off steam eases the strain on the boiler. Perhaps simply because of the incidence of occasional good shots, when the adrenaline of anger changes to that of happiness and the golfer is at peace.

> In peaceful thought the field of death surveyed,
> To fainting squadrons sent the timely aid,
> Inspir'd repuls'd battalions to engage,
> And taught the doubtful battle where to rage.

Some day an eminent alienist may write a book on the subject. I should be glad to supply him with innumerable case-histories, my own included.

The late Rev.Tom Allan held the same view. Tom was one of the hardest working and most powerful preachers that Scotland has ever produced. For a time he led the 'Tell Scotland' evangelical campaign with huge success. In his early years, as he himself confessed to me, he was inclined to drink heavily as an antidote to worry and anxiety. As a result he became an alcoholic. But after World War II, while working in Paris with Military Intelligence, he heard an American Negro singing 'Were You There?' at a church service and was at once converted to the Christian faith. He still found his struggle against alcoholism a difficult one; but not long afterwards he discovered golf as well as religion and, as he told me, the struggle became easier.

He was a first-class golfer in every sense (at one time he had a handicap of 3), and I remember well his 'day of glory', as he called it, when, playing with two other addicts and myself, he had a hole in one at the 14th at Dunaverty. Afterwards we had the usual celebration. He made no objection to us having a drink, but he himself would accept nothing stronger than orange juice. 'If I had one dram,' he said, 'I should be liable to have a dozen.' Though dormant, the temptation remained alive and vicious. I believe, with all due reverence, that God and golf gave him the strength to conquer it.

On the physical side, doctors may prescribe golf simply because of the regular exercise it entails and the lungfuls of fresh air a player requires not only to swing clubs and climb steep sand-dunes but also to utter comments on his own game in as forceful a manner as possible.

Sir William Schwenck Gilbert (otherwise W.S.Gilbert) wrote some lines which may be considered apposite:

> Roll on, thou ball, roll on!
> Through fathomless realms of space.
>> Roll on!
> What though I'm in a sorry case?
> What though I cannot meet my bills?
> What though I suffer toothache's ills?
> What though I swallow countless pills?
>> Never *you* mind!
>> Roll on!

But within recent years the medical profession has questioned the health value of the golf game. (It has also questioned the health value of white bread, sugar, orange squash, parsnips, castor oil and even kissing; not to mention sex.) One medical 'expert' has pointed out that golf is good if practised regularly but bad if pursued only in desperate bouts at weekends. I am no judge of such a pronouncement. All I know is that golfers who reach the allotted span are usually fitter and happier than non-golfers of the same age.

And from this there emerges an important truth concerning golf. Rugby, soccer, tennis, swimming and rock climbing are, in the main, enjoyed only in the 'vaward of our youth'. But golf can be enjoyed at any age. There was a newspaper story in 1968 about a retired clergyman, the Rev. E.T.Kirby, who celebrated his ninety-seventh birthday by playing with two members at the Ashford Manor course. 'They put me down between shots!' he joked, dancing a little jig in the clubhouse afterwards.

A neighbour of mine played regular games over nine holes with a partner only a few years his junior, until one day, at the age of ninety-two, he came in from the course, had his tea, then expired peacefully in an armchair. His death was as neat and tidy as that of Bing Crosby, who died happily after winning a 'bounce' four-ball on the last green.

A retired farmer, my neighbour, was a *coiteach*, which is the Gaelic for a left-hander. His favourite club was a hickory-shafted mashie with a rusty head which he called 'the wee black fella'. With it he could almost always chip to the hole-side from any distance up to fifty yards. And his putting was deadly. Because of this, the young bloods at Dunaverty, who could outdrive him by the length of a football pitch, were always delighted to be drawn with him in a foursome competition. They had the length, he had the accuracy. Besides, he had a handicap of 18 which, when strokes were being given, offset their own single-figure ones.

There is no dodging the fact, however, that in some respects golf is dangerous. Some players – particularly tournament players – are prone to backache. Others become round-shouldered, a natural consequence of a crouching posture at the address. Henry Cotton is not only round-shouldered, he also walks with his left shoulder higher than the right, again owing to the way he stands to the ball.

Paradoxically, however, sufferers from minor disabilities – for example my diarrhoea, already cited – often play better as a result of their condition. Indeed, I know of otherwise honest men who, as they approach the first tee in a monthly medal, will actually invent an ailment to bolster their morale.

They also do it, of course, to provide themselves with an alibi should their plan go awry and they happen to play badly. They can also rationalize failure better than any spokesman for the Ministry of Defence, often bringing debility to their aid. But to understand all is to forgive all, and, in any case, they are deceiving nobody except themselves.

The history of golf is laden with stories of golfers who triumphed over ills, real or imaginary. When Henry Cotton won the Open at Sandwich in 1934 (and with a second round of 65 gave its name to a famous golf ball) he played the final eighteen holes with a stomach grievously upset by something he had eaten at lunch. Ben Hogan won the US Open in 1950 limping heavily after the car crash which almost put an end to his career. During the Pensacola Open in 1962 Doug Sanders stepped barefoot on a piece of glass in his hotel and gashed his foot, yet he won the competition with many shots to spare. When Ken Venturi became US Open Champion at Washington in 1964 he was so exhausted in the final round that he had to be helped off the 18th green by a doctor. Billy Casper, at one time leading money-winner on the US Circuit, was so prone to obscure ailments that in an effort to overcome them he lived for years on a diet of buffalo steaks and rattlesnake stew.

In the days preceding the 1982 Open at Royal Troon golf writers were less concerned with reporting practice scores than with assessing medical bulletins. Jack Nicklaus was recovering from a bout of gastric 'flu. Tom Weiskopf had a streaming cold. Lee Trevino's back was bothering him even after a course of acupuncture. Tom Watson's pinkie was inflamed and sore. As soon as I heard about that pinkie I was fairly certain that Tom Watson was going to win. Which he duly did.

In my own club, Dunaverty, I have golfing friends who in

private life enjoy the rudest of health but on the golf course acquire unfortunate diseases. Fibrositis, sciatica, lumbago and tennis elbow are perhaps the most common, but mention is also frequently made of sinusitis, bronchitis and ulcers, both duodenal and gastric. These latter always seem to manifest themselves towards the end of a game, particularly if the sufferer has put his ball in the river at the 17th and gone dormie one down. A regular opponent of mine who, in normal circumstances, can identify a bottle of Islay Mist at a distance of a hundred yards, has been known to plead incipient blindness.

Though a professing Christian and thus expected to demonstrate love and care for my neighbours, I have learned by experience that to betray Christian feelings on the golf course is almost always a mistake. When the Colonel sighs and wipes the rain from his glasses – 'My sight is going, Angus. Soon I may have to give up golf altogether!' – I utter no heartfelt expression of sorrow, because I know his eyesight is keener than a hawk's and that in the next few seconds he is going to sink a long putt and win the hole.

When the Sheriff staggers down the sandy path to the 15th tee, using his driver as a limping stick, and says: 'I'm getting too old for this, Angus. My legs are going!' I refuse to offer him a supporting arm (even though he *is* seventy-nine), because I know he is about to hit a spanking drive straight down the middle of the fairway and smile complacently as I hook wildly into the whins.

When the retired headmaster complains of the bitter cold – 'So bad for my chest, Angus' – and even chitters audibly on the 1st tee, I spare him no sympathy, because I know he is going to outdrive me by many yards and has found a method – which does not work for me – of avoiding the dreaded 'yips'.

Perhaps the most serious danger to a golfer is a loss of temper. The old Scots pro who once told me, 'Keep the heid still, son, an' even mair important, keep the heid!' pointed unerringly towards the truth. Bad temper during a game – always, of course, directed against yourself – can lead to boils, spots before the eyes, high blood pressure and apoplexy. It can also be fatal.

Take the case of one Michael Scaglione, reported by Martin Dunn of the *Sunday Express*, in 1982.

His temper on the golf course was notorious. He would hurl his putter into the lake after a bad putt, wildly hit his ball in any direction after slicing or hooking a drive and curse at the top of his voice after the smallest of errors.

Over the three years he had been a member of the Sun Creek Golf Club near New Orleans, so many members had backed away from playing with him that he often had to go round by himself.

However, when Michael arrived at the course for an afternoon round one day last week he found three members looking for another player to make up a foursome. Despite his reputation they allowed Michael to join them, and for ten holes his behaviour was impeccable.

That all changed on the 11th tee when Michael sliced his drive so badly that the ball shot off at right angles with the tee and was lost in a clump of thick bushes. In an uncontrolled burst of temper Michael ranted and raved and hurled his club against the nearby motorized caddy cart.

But he threw it with such force that the club head snapped off and the broken shaft bounced back, its jagged end piercing Michael's jugular vein like a spear. He died on his way to hospital.

On the whole, however, golf cannot be classed as danger-ous. In the physical sense, at any rate. 'It is a great game,' Tony Jacklin once told my son, Jock, 'despite all the troughs and travail. It is an education in itself, if sometimes a painful one. I know of no other recreation which is a better character builder.'

After sixty happy years of golf – with more to come, I hope – I can support Tony's statement. I believe he over-empha-sizes the pain and the 'troughs and travail', but this may be because he is a professional, playing for money. An amateur plays for pleasure and can, therefore, afford to be more philosophical when a temporary deterioration in form occurs. His mind is also more open to suggestion during his many long conferences with his Creator. (Incidentally, according to the Rules of Golf, the only opponent from whom you can seek advice *is* your Creator.)

For myself, I should like to supplement Tony's definition

with the idea that being a golfer is like being in love. There is the agony and the ecstasy, with one moment of ecstasy worth a hundred of agony.

I am not sure if Jean, my wife, agrees with me. I was eleven years old when I met her, at about the same time as I became a golfer. Jock took up the game at an even earlier age and now travels the world reporting it. Jean suffers us both patiently, however, and it may be that she finds a grain of truth in my idea.

MEMO

Your bad days at golf are not at all serious to your fellow players. If anything, each of your bad shots builds the other fellow's ego. Don't apologize and don't tell how good you were last Saturday. Just let your day's bad golf slide . . . You can't alibi a 100 score down to 80.

Don Harold

3. Gallowses are Good for You

I became a golfer at the age of eleven in order to avoid being sent to a dancing class.

Having spent one session with Mr McLeish and his daughter, who conducted a School of Dancing near Charing Cross in Glasgow but came in the summer to teach in our various small communities in Kintyre, I had reached the conclusion – a conclusion shared by many of my schoolfriends but not, unfortunately, by my parents – that as a dancer I had as much chance of success as a three-toed sloth.

In a way I regretted this, because at the class the previous year I had been given as a partner a small, dainty creature, aged nine, called Jean McKerral, in whom I found myself taking a peculiar interest. At the Grand Display of Dancing which brought the session to a close my main contribution to the programme was to act as a statue in the Statue Dance – one arm outstretched, the other akimbo – and the only sustaining influence against the ribald cat-calls of my mates at the back of the hall was the sight of her dancing around me, as light and accurate as a golf ball chipped on to the green by Joyce Wethered. But even the thought of Jean proved no match for my juvenile belief that dancing was a pastime for cissies and that outdoor pursuits were more appropriate for young energetic males.

One of my schoolmates was Hamish Taylor, whose nickname, for no apparent reason, was Boskers. He is now Lt.-Col. Hamish Taylor, MC, OBE, formerly Convener of Argyll County Council but still a faithful golfer. His father was a farmer, one of the original members of Dunaverty Golf Club, founded in 1888, and from him Boskers had acquired a few old clubs and balls. I told my father about this, and he said: 'All right, you can borrow my blasted mashie and my blasted putter, but you'll have to find your own blasted balls.' (I discovered later why, at the time, his temper was even more brittle than usual and no balls were forthcoming. He had lost six in a recent medal competition.)

Boskers took pity on my poverty. After showing me how to hold and swing my father's mashie, he gave me an old ball with which to practise. The first shot I hit properly covered nearly fifty yards. I shouted with joy. Boskers sneered, addressed a much whiter ball with a wooden club and sent it soaring twice as far. Having thus demonstrated his superiority, he advised me that the next time I tried to play golf I ought to borrow my father's driver rather than his mashie. Then, he said, I might be able to achieve a length almost, if not quite, as prodigious as his own.

But I wasn't jealous. I had discovered the wonderful feeling that comes from a well-struck golf shot. The virus had entered my system. Ever since it has enjoyed long and satisfying meals of my blood.

It was at this stage that I persuaded my parents that instead of becoming a dancer I ought to combine healthful exercise with good fresh air and become a golfer. My mother, in her quiet way, was disappointed, but my father, being at the time a golfer himself, was reasonably happy with the arrangement.

From one of his elders, whose arthritis had caused him to give up the game, he got three old hickory-shafted clubs for me: a brassie, a mashie and a putter.

With that mashie I learned to perform wonders — long approaches, bunker shots, chips to the green – which I find difficult to emulate today even with the superb Ben Hogan 7-iron (Producer Model) which came via Arthur Thomson, Machrihanish, from John Panton's shop at Glenbervie. But I had poor success in playing the brassie, probably because the shaft was too long for a boy, and when I tried to shorten my grip its extremity became entangled in my clothing. (I think it is important that boys and girls who contract the virus should be supplied at first with clubs cut down to size, so that an easy, natural swing can be developed at an early stage.)

As for the putter, it is still there, in the garage. I keep it hanging on the wall, in much the same way as an ageing ancestor of mine might have kept his claymore to remind him of clan battles past and gone. At eleven years old – and uninhibited – I could putt as well as Boskers and all the other boys, which was very well indeed. Nowadays . . . But that is another story.

In summer Boskers and I played in our bare feet. His parents and mine provided us both with sandshoes, but as our contemporaries at school and on the course were mainly from poorer families in the village, for whom such exotic footgear – even at half-a-crown a pair – was too expensive, in the way of all boys we were determinedly conformist, not to say democratic, and cultivated leather-hard feet like the others.

Nowadays, when, ignominiously, I take off my shoes and socks to retrieve a ball from the burn at the 17th, I always play the next pitch to the green in my bare feet. The old thrill returns, and it is an odd fact that nine times out of ten I execute a near-perfect shot. More evidence, I suppose, that golf is as much a mental as a physical exercise.

Boskers and I also played in 'gallowses'. It was lucky for us that Dunaverty had no rules about appropriate attire like the Yorkshire course I visited between the wars which had a notice on the clubhouse door: PLAYING IN BRACES IS FORBIDDEN.

At the time, more than sixty years ago, belts for boys were not fashionable in remote Scottish parishes like Southend at the Mull of Kintyre. This may have been because, as a rule, our short trousers were made by our mothers, more often than not from garments discarded by fathers and older brothers and designed, therefore, to be supported by braces. I remember my mother making 'gallowses' for me out of strips from a red flannel petticoat of her own, with buttonhole straps taken from old ones belonging to my father.

As I grew older and was able to buy trousers of my own, I still played golf in my 'gallowses', being convinced that a belt might interfere with the smoothness of my swing. (I have been told by friends – and even close relatives – that never in living memory have I possessed a smooth swing: that, in fact, the one I do possess resembles nothing so much as the action of a mad hammer-thrower at a Highland Games. Such comment, of course, is irrelevant. If a faithful golfer *believes* he has a smooth swing, then the results will be satisfactory: to him, at any rate. It is one of the mystical truths of the game.)

I played in braces until after World War II, when it became almost impossible to buy ready-made trousers *without* belts and the cost of having a pair made to my own specifications went far beyond my means. By that time, however, army service had freed me from finicky superstitions and I began to believe that I could swing just as well wearing a belt as I could wearing braces.

At times, however, my conversion was 'clouded with a doubt'. One day I was playing in a local competition with Hughie Sinclair, who, as custodian of the Ladies' course at the neighbouring Machrihanish Club, had a wide knowledge of life and golf. As I drove off from the 1st tee he jolted my concentration by remarking, casually: 'Angus, ye've nae sweevil at a'!'

In a moment of panic I considered there and then the possibility of buying a new pair of trousers, with buttons for 'gallowses'. But as the game went on there occurred to me a niggling suspicion that Hughie's remark had not been so much a statement of fact as a subtle form of gamesmanship. The thought was so distasteful that it caused my golf to deteriorate into banality, and it was a relief when a rainstorm, accompanied by thunder and lightning, struck us at the 8th hole (*Bruaich Mor*), where, by mutual consent, we decided to abandon the game. Later, in the clubhouse bar, under the influence of a few enjoyable drams, we forgot about 'sweevils' and gamesmanship and were comrades again.

Golfers, of course, like authors and actors, are susceptible to superstition. One of my regular partners at Dunaverty would never dream of starting a game without touching a small silver medal which nestles among the tees in his right-hand trouser pocket. He won it in a Stableford Competition some forty years ago and, despite the daunting knowledge that he has never won a competition since, he believes it brings him luck.

Another old friend of mine – now unhappily no longer with

us – used to swear that he could play his best golf only after a substantial plate of stewed rhubarb. Perhaps his idea was similar to that of Lee Trevino, who once, as he stood on the first tee in an important tournament, remarked in a loud voice to an appreciative audience: 'Normally I say a hungry dog hunts better. But this morning I had a good breakfast. On a full stomach butterflies do not have room to fly.'

An acquaintance of Gerald Micklem once told me that if Gerald begins a round wearing rain-proofs he will keep them on until he has holed his last putt on the 18th green, even though, in the meantime, the sun has emerged and he has become liable to heat exhaustion. He is afraid that if he discards them his swing may lose its rhythm. (Mind you, unlike some golfers who could be named, Gerald Micklem has a rhythm to lose.)

Jack Nicklaus has confessed that he always plays with three pennies in his pocket. And when he marks his ball on the green with one of them he does it tails up.

My wife's former pin-up boy, Peter Thomson (now succeeded in her affections by Greg Norman), used to wear a copper bracelet on an arthritic wrist. For all I know he may wear it still. He was presented with it by a white hunter in Zimbabwe (then Rhodesia) who believed in the 'copper cure' for rheumatic ailments, although doctors describe the 'copper cure' as plain superstition.

Jock tells me that the bold and bouncing Severiano Ballesteros refuses to play with a ball numbered 3, because, in his belief, it psyches him into three-putting. I have always suspected that behind Seve's insouciance there lurks a vein of gloomy self-doubt.

In my own case, I always put on my left golf-shoe before my right. It must be confessed, however, that this superstition occurs also in my everyday life. Each morning, for the past sixty years, I have reached first for my left shoe, boot or · wellington.

The custom was acquired after I had read *Saint Columba of Iona* by Lucy Menzies. From this fascinating book I learned that my ancestors in a tribe called the Scotti, who came from Ireland some two thousand years ago to people the mainland of Scotland, had always done things from left to right – things such as putting on their leather *brogans* (footgear) or marching round a stone cairn as they prepared for battle. The idea originated, of course, in the Druidical concept of a sun-god: a god which rose in the east each morning and moved across the sky from left to right. Doing anything in the opposite direction – *widdershins*, as they called it – was inviting trouble from evil spirits.

So, as a kind of insurance, I put on my left golf-shoe first. There are plenty of evil spirits abroad on a golf course without risking the advent of a few more.

MEMO

Ye see, Professor, as lang as ye are learnin' thae lads at the College Latin and Greek it is easy work, but when ye come tae play golf ye maun hae a heid.

Lang Willie, a St Andrews caddy

4. Men, Women and Clergymen

St Columba, if not specifically a golfer, was an enthusiastic shinty player. A shinty player, moreover, inclined to be unrepentant when he hacked a monkish opponent on the shin. This is made plain by his biographer, Adomnan.

He loved his fellow men; and he loved children in particular, as is evident from a little poem he has bequeathed to us:

> O conscience clear,
> O soul unsullied,
> Here is a kiss for thee –
> Give thou a kiss to me.

He was gentle with ordinary sinners but brought down terrible curses upon those he termed 'the smug hypocrites'. He gave women an honourable place in society, ignoring a social structure in which they were regarded almost as chattels. (In his day, of course, there were no lady golfers.) In Iona, where an Abbey now stands on the site of his sixth-century cell, he founded the first animal hospital known to history, and the story is told of a crane with a broken leg which he nursed back to full health. (I am sure that if he broke an opponent's leg at shinty he would be similarly concerned and attentive.)

St Columba was a churchman, a statesman, a poet and a sportsman. Above all, a human being, whose halo tended to be 'a kennin crooked'. For me, he seems to have had all the characteristics of a faithful golfer, and I have often wondered if, in his day, he might indeed have tried out a few golf shots.

Iona has all the makings of a good course, though as yet it lies untouched by the hand of a developer. Smooth green machair-land above sandy beaches, some of it intersected by small streams. Clumpy rough, made punitive by tufts of bog myrtle. Marshy ground, the home of many kingcups, which could be fairly classified as casual water. Larks singing in the clear air. Surely on a bright summer's morning, St Columba must often have been tempted to challenge his disciples to long-hitting competitions with their shinty sticks, or *camans*, as he would call them in his native Gaelic.

I can imagine him, having driven straight down the middle and being well set up for a short pitch to the nominated boulder, giving his 'beloved Kenneth' a straight look as the latter finds his ball deep among the bog myrtle and inquires humbly if he may have a lift. 'Not at all,' is the holy one's stern reply. 'Play it where it lies, my boy!' (And in the holy heart beneath the monkish habit a satisfying thought: 'In a minute I'm going to be one up!')

If St Columba was a golfer, then he was only the first of a long line of clergymen devoted to the game. In many a clubhouse today, on a Monday morning – 'Ministers' Monday' – dog collars can be seen hanging by the dozen in the locker-room, while their owners, temporarily enjoying release from grace and piety, hook and slice their various ways around the course.

Is there material for a psychologist in the widespread desire among clergymen to play golf? Does the game provide them with a modern equivalent of the hair shirt? Do they recognize that a constant exercising of the discipline and strict honesty required of every faithful golfer improves the condition of their immortal souls? Or is golf a kind of spiritual safety-valve for men (and women) whose calling prevents them, in ordinary circumstances, from showing aggression in action or speech?

I must admit that with the exception of my late father and my brother, who ministers to a parish in Perthshire, I have never heard a clergyman swear out loud while playing golf. Tom Allan, that lovely man and golfer, would sometimes mutter the expletive 'Yam!' if a shot of his went astray, which was seldom. But, as his eyes flashed, I always had the feeling that he meant something else. John R. Gray, ex-Moderator of the General Assembly of the Church of Scotland, goes round Dunaverty roaring abuse at himself, but his abuse consists of exotic and little-known Scots words and is accompanied by smiles indicating priestly self-discipline.

On the other hand, I have never come across a golfing clergyman who showed the slightest surprise or indignation at hearing a partner or an opponent swear. This may be because a minister is never likely to forget the words of the Lord's Prayer: 'Forgive us our debts as we forgive our debtors.' The late Henry Longhurst, that entertaining recorder of golf history, told the following story, implying that his experience with clergymen was similar to mine.

Many, many years ago, I was playing in a Bedfordshire Northants Alliance meeting in company with a partnership consisting of the then vicar of Northampton and a gentleman whose complexion indicated either good living or shortness of temper, or both. They were doing rather well, and at the 17th were in with a definite chance. At this point the vicar's partner had only to loft a short pitch over the bunker on to the green, when, alas, up came his head, out came a lump of turf, and the ball dropped feebly into the bunker. The man lifted his niblick to heaven. ' – – – – !' he cried, and ' – – – – !' and ' – – – – !' Then pulling himself up with a jerk, he began to make embarrassed apologies. The vicar's reply remains in my mind as though it were yesterday. 'Brother,' he said, slowly and gently, 'the provocation was ample.'

I have always argued that a clergyman partner can be of immense value in a 'bounce' four-ball. Your opponents tend to be inhibited in their speech and actions. Tension builds up inside them as they stifle their usual loud and violent methods of exorcizing disappointment. And tension, as every golfer knows, is the ultimate enemy of good golf.

I once played over Dunaverty with another Moderator, Hugh Douglas, actually during his year of office. He was – and still is – a faithful and more than competent golfer. He and I played a match against formidable opponents in the persons of Donald McDiarmid, then Sheriff-Substitute of Argyll, and my old friend, Boskers. As I watched them play the occasional indifferent shot and then struggle not only to discipline their language but also to maintain their normal urbane conversation and behaviour, the feeling came to me that Hugh and I were on to a good thing.

And so it proved. The match ended on the 15th green with sporting handshakes but with our opponents' complexions verging on the apoplectic. As we went towards the 16th tee to play the first hole of the bye, Hugh's eyes were twinkling with a certain smug satisfaction. 'Perhaps it wasn't fair, Angus,' he remarked, glancing upwards. 'You and I had a hot line.'

I have mentioned my brother Kenneth, known to many of his parishioners in Kenmore, where he has ministered (and golfed) since 1950, as the 'Bishop of Loch Tayside'. He tells a story which well illustrates my views on clerical golfers.

Though in his sixties, Kenneth is slim and youthful-looking. His aspect of worldliness makes him appear, without his dog-collar, more like an alert businessman than a pious clergyman. He provides, in fact, positive evidence of my contention that behind almost every dog-collar there is a human being (and perhaps also a faithful golfer) struggling to get out.

One day he was playing in a pro-am competition with Alex Mitchell, then the Taymouth Castle professional, against a partnership consisting of another professional and a somewhat happy-go-lucky young amateur. Their opponents were golfing brilliantly, despite the fact that the amateur accompanied certain of his shots with boisterous swear-words indicating, impartially, joy and sorrow.

Though somewhat inhibited by the success achieved by this less than faithful golfer, Alex Mitchell continued to converse with him in friendly terms and discovered, to his surprise, that he came from Kintyre, where Kenneth was born. With a smile which must have contained an element of evil intent, Alex said: 'What a coincidence! You and my partner coming from the same neck of the woods. You'll know the name. He is the Rev. Kenneth MacVicar, Minister of Menmore.' A flush spread over the young man's face. 'Oh, God,' he whispered, 'what have I been saying?'

From that moment, as my saintly brother relates with unsaintly glee, the poor man's game went to pieces, and

Kenneth and his professional went on to win one of the main prizes.

One advantage enjoyed by golfing clergymen could be the benefit they receive from their 'hot line' along the fairways. Some of them, I reckon, are inclined to be a trifle smug about this aspect of their sporting situation.

During his youthful ministry the Rev. Andrew B.McLellan of St Andrews spent a holiday in Southend and was booked by my father to conduct a Sunday morning service. He was – and, I hope, still is – a keen golfer, who loved a game with plenty of fun in it, not to say gamesmanship. On the Saturday evening he and my brother Kenneth played against Boskers and myself and beat us on the last green, where, with our divine opponents behind me apparently both struck by a sudden attack of whooping-cough, I yipped – and missed – a two-yard putt to save the match.

Next morning, as the Rev. Andrew delivered his prayer of intercession from the pulpit of St Blaan's, I suddenly became alert. 'And now,' he intoned, in a voice suddenly heavy with unction, 'we pray for the sportsmen in our midst, who are in a unique position to know that the race is not always to the swift nor the battle to the strong and who can accept without envy the fact that in the good game (*pause*) of life (*pause*) some are more gifted than others.'

I hoped, viciously but vainly I have no doubt, that on his next round over Dunaverty he would visit every evil hazard on the course.

My father, however, was a notable exception to the 'hot line' theory. If he had one, it clearly became disconnected when he set foot on a golf course. Indeed, he was defeated by golf, due mainly, I am afraid, to his lack of proper tempera-ment for the game. An essential element in the make-up of a golfer is humble patience, and my father was neither humble nor patient. He was a fine pastor and preacher but a menace on the links.

During World War I he served for a time as chaplain with the Lovat Scouts, mainly in Salonika, which was why he became known to all his friends and acquaintances (and to his own family) as the Padre. Some time after he retired in 1957, after having laboured spiritually in Southend for forty-seven years, the BBC made a film about him entitled 'The Old Padre'. It dealt with his faithful ministry in a rural community and with his many contributions to public service as a Presbytery Clerk, County Councillor and Justice of the Peace. But it made no mention of his golf. I took care of that. I wrote the script.

Part of the trouble was that as a boy in North Uist and then as a divinity student at Glasgow University he had been an excellent shinty player. Indeed, he became the first captain of the Glasgow University Shinty Club when it was founded in 1901 and played for Scotland against Ireland in several international matches. (Two of his granddaughters, Susan and Marsali, have played hockey for Scotland. He was intensely proud when reports of their skill began to appear in the newspapers. Before he died in 1970, at the age of ninety-two, he was in the habit of announcing to all and sundry: 'Heredity, of course. They take it from me!')

I think he expected that having been good at shinty he would be good at golf as well. What he failed to understand was that while learning to play shinty is like learning to play the drums, learning to play golf is like learning to play the violin. For the drums you need aggression and even a hint of violence. For the violin you need a loving patience and a delicate sense of touch.

Delicate was not a word ever used in the context of my father's golf. The man who stood nobly in the pulpit on a Sunday, preaching love and goodwill to all mankind, became, on a Monday, on the golf course, a desperate creature full of hate. Hate for the ball at which he stared down so savagely. Hate for the clubs he whirled so high above his head. And hate, apparently, for the very ground he stood on as he struck huge divots out of it.

At school I had been introduced to Shakespeare's 'Scotch Play' and had found in it lines which I thought might well have applied to the Padre as a golfer.

Disdaining fortune, with his brandished steel,
Which smoked with bloody execution,
Like valour's minion carved out his passage.

(Forty years later, when steel shafts had finally displaced all the old hickory ones, a memory of the same lines recurred to me as I watched Arnold Palmer's swashbuckling though ultimately vain pursuit of Kel Nagle in the Centenary Open at St Andrews in 1960.)

The Padre found much pleasure and satisfaction in playing shinty. In golf he found none. He was like a man whose wife had left him: a man who turns for comfort to a cool and sophisticated call-girl and discovers, in anguish, that professional love-making brings no satisfaction.

Some men, I suppose, are able to come to terms with such a situation and adapt their life-style to it. But not my father, who was simple and direct in thought and action. If golf couldn't be played like shinty, then golf was not for him. He took several years to make the decision. It occurred in a dramatic way during an Autumn Meeting at Dunaverty.

That morning he had asked me to caddy for him. Or, rather, he had commanded me to caddy for him, the humble word 'ask' being rare in his vocabulary. I remember standing with his bag outside the clubhouse door. It was blowing a near-gale and pelting with rain. The thought of accompanying my father as he played eighteen holes in such conditions caused me deep misgivings, and it wasn't altogether the weather that was worrying me. And when he emerged at last with his partner my worries multiplied. His partner was a local farmer with a caustic tongue, with whom, for years, he had carried on political strife.

The Padre's first shot went off the toe of his club into the corn-field bordering part of the first fairway.

'Three aff the tee,' said his partner.

'I know the rules,' said my father, grinding his teeth.

With the rain glistening on his slightly bald head and dripping from his red moustache, but with dog-collar still firmly in place, he stood up to his second ball like a Viking chief with a sore throat confronting a Pictish enemy. His driver head was thrust up almost perpendicularly, it was looped and swung in the style of a shinty player, it was pulled down and through in a blur of speed against a left leg suddenly, aggressively stamped forward and down. 'Ah-h-h!' exclaimed the Padre, as the ball, momentarily flattened by the terrible blow, flew straight down the fairway for about 300 yards. Did I see wisps of steam coming from the raindrops as that 'oak-cleaving thunderbolt' hurtled through them? In that short space of time I was proud of my father.

His partner made no comment other than a loud sniff. He put a canny drive down the middle. In spite of the wind and the rain he got his next on the green and had a par 4.

My father foozled his fourth shot, angrily stabbed the next one over the green, tried and failed to putt another through some longish grass and finished with a 9.

'It's the weather!' he snarled at me, as I offered him a club on the 2nd tee. 'And what's this?' he demanded, glancing at a driver I had taken from his bag. 'I don't need a driver at this hole!'

'It's over 200 yards and against the wind,' I reasoned with him.

'What do you know about it! Give me my cleek.'

The ageing farmer took his driver. His shot, though straight, was still many yards short of the green.

'There you are,' I said.

My father's fingers worked in clenching motions, possibly like the fingers of the Boston Strangler. But he refrained from harming me. He wiped the rain from his face and savagely attacked his ball with the cleek. It flew high and wide, carried on the wind, and was last seen heading for the troubled waters of Machribeg Bay.

'I see ye're inclined tae gang left even on the golf course,' remarked his partner, with political intent. 'That'll be three aff the tee again.'

It was only later when I became a faithful golfer, that I began to understand the amount of self-restraint exercised by my father during most of that round. After his outburst against my judgement on the 2nd tee he maintained a grim silence.

Driving from the 5th tee he put two balls into the river in

succession. His partner observed, casually: 'Ye're aye prayin'
for the likes o' us. Maybe if ye tried a prayer for yersel ye
micht get ower the burn.'

Still he said nothing. In the circumstances neither did I.

The rain went off at about the 15th hole, which runs
alongside the same river. By that time we were all soaked to
the skin. I was suffering with my father. But I was also made
unhappy by his apparent lack of sympathy for my wetness and
by his inimical attitude when I lagged behind and he had to
wait for his clubs before he could play a shot. I suspect, too,
that a terrible frustration was building inside him as the old
farmer continued to play steadily and, indeed, threatened to
break his handicap.

It was at the 17th hole that the overheated boiler finally
burst. Using a mashie for his third shot, the Padre attempted
to hoist his ball across the river. Turf flew and a double splash
occurred as ball and divot disappeared together beneath the
turgid tide. 'What a peety!' said his partner, apparently
without emotion.

Even in the cold, damp atmosphere my father's face was
coloured a deep and dangerous red. With gallant self-control,
however, he put down another ball and prepared to attempt a
second approach shot. 'Ye're supposed tae drap it ower yer
left shoother,' said the old farmer.

A strangled sound came from my father's mouth. 'Give me
my card!' he shouted at his partner.

The card was immediately forthcoming. He tore it in
pieces. He lifted his ball. He snatched the bag of clubs from
my weakening grip. Then, using his shinty swing, he hurled
card shreds, ball and bag into the river. 'Wade in for them,' he
said to me. 'From now on they're yours.'

His partner won the Autumn Meeting. I was told that at the
prize-giving the old farmer made a speech. 'I was playin' wi'
the meenister,' he said. 'He gi'ed me inspiration!'

But 'the meenister' never played competitive golf again.
That night, after saying his prayers and composing himself,
with difficulty, to sleep, did the words of Shakespeare in
Love's Labour's Lost occur to him?

Why, all delights are vain; but that most vain,
Which, with pain purchas'd, doth inherit pain.

He was faithful in his care for the old and the sick. Young people in trouble came to him for guidance, unafraid. As he grew older his reputation for simple integrity flourished. With the strong aid of my mother he brought up his family to appreciate Christian codes of conduct and to respect the divinity in every human being. You could say that he possessed many of the attributes of a golfer, and I think you would be right. But his Creator had other plans for him and, in his case, omitted to supply him with the catalytic ingredients necessary in a faithful golfer's character. He found it difficult to curb impatience. He did not love golf for its own sake and, therefore, failed to enjoy it when playing badly. Importantly, he had no taste for black comedy.

And yet the Padre was never critical of golfers or golf, because, at heart, he was a sportsman. Boldly he took the side of a colleague, the Rev. George Walter Strang of Campbeltown, who once found himself in trouble for having played golf instead of attending a Presbytery meeting.

The Rev. George, like Boskers's father, was one of the founder members of Dunaverty Golf Club. Indeed, the first hole on our course is called after him: 'Strang's'. He was strong and stocky, with a sharp little grey beard and, at times, an irascible manner. He was such a straight-shooter in a moral sense (as well as on the golf course) that were he alive today he might have been nicknamed John Wayne.

He was more than a little absent-minded. On one occasion, perhaps because his putting had let him down that afternoon and he was worrying about it, he forgot a wedding date. A messenger came rushing to the manse door to remind him, and in sore distress he pulled on his coat, put on his hat and stumped rapidly down the Main Street to make amends. Bursting into the house, he saw the young couple, the best man and bridesmaid standing in a row before him. 'Tell me,' he panted, 'which of you is the father of the child?'

He had two ruling passions. One was for the welfare of the poor in his parish, and I well remember him growling to my

father: 'What's the good of praying with people unless you fill
their stomachs first!' The other was for golf. On both counts
he was often criticized; but his habit was to dismiss such
criticism with piratical snarls.

Then came the day when he stood up before the Presbytery
accused of playing truant from a meeting in order to indulge
in a game of golf. Adding to the enormity of his 'crime' was
the fact that the game had been with his bosom crony, the
local Roman Catholic priest. Protestant wrath eddied round
him like the odour of weed-killer on an infested green.

But the Rev. George spoke spiritedly in his own defence.
'It was a lovely day,' he said, 'ideal for beneficial exercise, and
surely the health and strength of a minister is important to his
congregation – and to the Presbytery. As for playing with the
priest, he is a very nice man. We may differ in details of our
religion, but we are both Christians who believe in God.'

In the end, after a speech in his defence by the Rev.
A. J. MacVicar, Presbytery Clerk, he got away with a mild
admonition. Happily he continued to play golf with the priest.

I have always found that golf is a powerful aid to
ecumenicalism in every aspect of life. If all our world
statesmen (and stateswomen) were faithful golfers, then
swords might be turned into sand-irons and nuclear bombs
into high-velocity golf balls.

MEMO

Statisticians estimate that crime among good golfers is lower than in
any class of the community except possibly bishops.

P.G. Wodehouse

5. Hickory, Hackery, Haskell

Not long after I began to play golf with my father's clubs – in 1919 it was – I fell from a tree and sprained my left arm. I had already sprained my right arm in a similar accident while my father was absent during the war. In consequence, the cultivation of my swing in those early years was inhibited. Indeed, I have never been able to strike the ball, as all faithful golfers should, with a perfectly straight left arm and with the right tucked fairly closely and comfortably into the side.

Today I get pains in both my elbows (not to mention hips), and when my golf is poor I can make rheumatism a ready excuse to anyone who cares to listen. Few do listen. Why should they? They all have troubles of their own. But it is fortunate that at any rate I am able to make excuses to myself. While exercising such convenient self-therapy, however, I have to block out of my memory, pro tem, the fact that in 1954, at Baltusrol, Ed Furgol won the US Open Championship. He, as my Creator always tends to remind me, had a withered arm.

For Boskers and myself, as we reached towards adolescence, the chief end of golf was to hit the ball as far as possible. He could always outdrive me. He still can, though as time goes on his tee-shots with wood are becoming shorter and shorter. The unfortunate thing is, so are mine.

Not long ago I was chatting with my young friend, Dr Marjory MacSween. About golf, of course. Her swing is impeccable and I play frequently with her husband, Professor Roddy MacSween, as enthusiastic about golf as he is about diseases of the liver, and so well balanced both morally and mentally that his most violent expletive, when he misses a short putt, consists of words bordering on the biblical:

'Scunnerations of Ezekiel!' I mentioned to Marjory an article I had read by Henry Cotton, in which he stated (Henry does not suggest: he states) that after the age of forty a man's drive loses two yards' distance every year. (Henry may have been quoting a remark made originally by the great Irish amateur, Dr Flaherty, but no matter: golfers share wisdom among themselves as clergymen, doctors and lawyers do.) Marjory looked at me with those eyes whose innocent brightness I have always had reason to suspect since she was handle-high to a caddy-car and said: 'Angus, you must be a minus quantity by now!'

Her estimate was close enough to the truth to be salutary. My objective, from that moment on, has been to prove Henry Cotton wrong and maintain the length I have. This is about 160 yards when I achieve a proper strike with a breeze in my favour, and perhaps 130 yards against a stiff sou'westerly. At times Bosker can better such distances by a few yards, though in both our cases satisfactory results can be obtained only when rheumatic pains are in abeyance.

But at a time when youth and blood were warmer, if our drives fell short of 250 yards we were disappointed. And confidence in our power was so overweening that if our elders played mid-irons through the green we always tried to match them with our mashies. On most occasions we failed. We still had not learned that golf has much less to do with brute strength than with acquired skill.

Of course, as boys beginning to play the game, we had to use equipment which made it impossible for us, at first, to hit the ball even as far as we do now. Our clubs were all shafted with hickory, and matched sets did not exist. Balls were old and scuffed: ones we had found among the bent on the course, ones we had discovered in odd corners at home, ones presented to us by our mates, so decrepit as to be unsaleable to adults. Tee pegs, spiked shoes and golf gloves were unknown.

It seems to me, in retrospect, that there was only one club in my father's bag in which I had full confidence: a beautifully balanced mashie made by a gentleman called Ralph Smith. Long ago I lent it to a friend and haven't seen it since. But I do still possess another of those ancient relics. It is kept in the umbrella stand inside our front door: a mid-iron with a head hand-forged by F. Munro of Prestwick. The hickory shaft is thick and heavy, apparently too thick and heavy for the smallish head. Like my father I could never hit a decent shot with it. Indeed, I thought nobody could, until one day my son Jock tried it out and surprised both of us with the result. But of course Jock's Creator, aided and abetted by that grand old teacher, the late Hector Thomson of Machrihanish, has blessed him with a swing of some elegance and power.

More than sixty years ago, when Boskers and I were emerging as faithful golfers, we played with a variety of balls, including 'woodies', 'gutties', 'floaters' and even some of the original Haskells. (After all, we had begun to operate less than twenty years after Dr Haskell, in America, had invented the first rubber-cored ball.) The only type of ball known in the history of golf that we didn't play was the 'feathery'.

I am told that the earliest golf-ball was the 'woodie', a wooden sphere of uncertain size. No doubt King James IV of Scotland regularly played with one, because a faded document records that in 1502 he purchased some 'clubbis and ballis' from the 'bowar of St Johnstown' – in more modern terms the bow-maker of Perth. This is the oldest written reference yet discovered to an individual golfer. And it indicates that the first golf clubs were probably made by highly skilled professional bow-makers.

Almost certainly, too, it was with a wooden ball that Mary, Queen of Scots – as far as I know the first lady golfer so mentioned by name – played a round on 'the fields beside Seton' only a few days after the murder of her husband, Darnley, at Kirk o' Fields in Edinburgh. I wonder if on 18 February 1584, as she was led to the scaffold, she took the mental escape route favoured by so many faithful golfers in distress and began counting to herself the number of putts she had taken on her last round? I can recommend this therapy to all worried businessmen and women threatened by sleeplessness. In my own case, lying abed at night, I seldom search back in memory even as far as the 12th green before sliding into oblivion.

History also supplies us with the identity of the first golf widow. When the great Marquis of Montrose got married in 1628, he played golf on the day before his wedding and, astonishingly, on the day after it. I think that at the time he must have been considerably worried about his game, because it is further recorded that nine days after the wedding he sent to St Andrews for more golf balls and 'six new clubbis' with which to replace the old ones.

What did the young Marchioness think about it all? History makes no mention of this. I hope that in common with most golf widows through the ages she was kind and understanding and comforted herself with the thought that being married to a golf addict was preferable to being saddled with an alcoholic or a rapist. I hope that she allowed him, like Desdemona with her Othello, 'often to beguile her of her tears' when he 'did speak of some distressful stroke'.

That Boskers and I, more than four hundred years after King James IV, should also be playing with 'woodies' is explained by the fact that during World War I golf balls were not being manufactured, at any rate on this side of the Atlantic, and they became so scarce that local joiners were persuaded to fashion a few for those afficionados too old for active service but still young enough to enjoy a game. When, after the war, rubber-cored balls reappeared on the market, the 'woodies' were discarded at once by the greybeards, but Boskers and I, chronically suffering from golf-ball starvation, were glad enough to get them.

The Golfers' Handbook records that during World War I a Wooden Ball Championship was played at Potchefstroom, South Africa, the winner being A. A. Horne of Potchefstroom, with a score of 90. I wonder if he was allowed to do as the elderly Dunaverty members did and tee up for every shot. If not, then his score over eighteen holes was remarkable. It has been said that with a brassie faced with balata belting a wooden ball could be driven a distance of 200 yards. I find this hard to believe. Boskers and I were lucky if we trundled one along for more than about the length of a cricket pitch.

The next ball in the evolution of the game was the 'feathery', which made its appearance in the early seventeenth century. This is the one type of ball of which Boskers and I had no practical knowledge. Though it could be struck farther than a 'woodie' and led to the fashioning of lighter and more easily handled clubs, it appears to have had certain disadvantages. Made from 'a top-hat full of steamed feathers sewn into a bull-hide casing', it was expensive and could be ruined by a single cut. In wet weather it became waterlogged and was inclined to split at the seams.

At the time, however, its advent created renewed enthusiasm for the game in Scotland. In *The Expedition of Humphry Clinker*, Tobias George Smollet (1721 – 1771) wrote almost lyrically about its virtues.

Hard by, in the fields called the links, the citizens of Edinburgh divert themselves at a game called Golf, in which they use a curious kind of bat tipped with horn, and small elastic balls of leather, stuffed with feathers, rather less than tennis balls, but of much harder consistency.

These they strike with such force and dexterity from one hole to another, that they will fly to an incredible distance. Of this diversion the Scots are so fond that, when the weather will permit, you may see a multitude of all ranks, from the senator of justice to the lowest tradesman, mingled together, in their shirts, and following the balls with the utmost eagerness.

Among others, I was shown one particular set of golfers, the youngest of whom was turned four-score. They were all gentlemen of independent fortunes, who had amused themselves with this pastime for the best part of a century without having ever felt the least alarm from sickness or disgust; and they never went to bed without having each the best part of a gallon of claret in his belly. Such uninterrupted exercise, co-operating with the keen air from the sea, must, without all doubt, keep the appetite always on edge, and steel the constitution against all the common attacks of distemper.

I like Tobias's last paragraph. With certain small emendations, such as the substitution of 'three score and ten' for 'four score' and of 'whisky and chasers' for 'claret', it could well be a description of the so-called 'geriatric four' at Dunaverty, of whom I am the eldest. We are often 'shown' to interested visitors as we hirple up the 18th fairway on a Saturday afternoon, intent upon being in time for the football results on the radio at five o'clock and our usual ham and egg tea at half-past.

In 1848 a curious incident occurred at St Andrews (where else?) which caused the 'feathery' to be superseded by a ball made of gutta percha. (According to *Chambers Twentieth Century Dictionary* gutta percha is the rubber-like juice of various trees in the Malayan jungle. It solidifies on exposure to the air.) In *The Game with the Hole in It*, Peter Dobereiner relates how a certain professor at the University, opening a crate addressed to him from the Far East, discovered that the statuette it contained had been protected on its journey by a packing of gutta percha. Curious about this greyish, gummy substance which he had never seen before, he rubbed a piece of it round and round between his hands. It hardened quickly, and in a moment of breathless wonder it came to him that he had made a golf ball.

The professor had a long handicap but was nevertheless a faithful golfer. He shared his discovery with some friends, and as they hacked about with the new gutty they learned, to their surprise, that the longer they played with it the better it flew. 'Students of dynamics,' writes Peter Dobereiner, no mean student of the subject himself, as far as it relates to golf, 'will require no further explanation. A perfectly smooth sphere makes a poor missile. But as the gutta percha balls became roughened by the impact of clubs, they responded to lift caused by eddying air over the indentations and flew straight and far.'

Then the professor's idea caught on. Gutties began to be sold by the professionals, their surfaces patterned to aid their flight. Some of them were made to resemble the 'feathery', with moulded seams and stitches. Others had bramble and lattice-work markings.

The bramble and lattice-work markings persisted long into the era of the rubber-cored ball. Indeed, it is only comparatively recently that balls patterned with lattice-work gave way to those in common use today, which had an arrangement of dimples found by the scientists to be the most effective.

The gutties played by Boskers and myself had lattice-work

markings. But they were so bruised and battered, when we came to use them, that it was difficult for us to discern any markings at all, apart from those caused by flailing niblicks. Not that at the time we were worried in the least about markings. Balls of whatever variety were there to be hit. So we hit them and they flew well enough for our purpose, which was to get them into the hole in fewer strokes than did our opponents.

Being cheaper, more durable and more available, the gutty caused a revolution in golf which lasted into the twentieth century. Its advent inspired a certain Dr William Graham – probably after completing an exceptionally good round, for him – to burst into verse:

> Hail! Gutta Percha, precious gum!
> O'er Scotland's links lang may ye bum.
> Some purse-proud billies haw and hum,
> And say ye're douf at fleein';
> But let them try ye fairly out
> Wi' ony balls for days about,
> Your merits they will loudly tout,
> And own they hae been leein'.

J. H. Taylor, Harry Vardon, Willie Auchterlonie, James Braid and Harold Hilton all won Open Championships playing 'gutties'. Their recorded four-round scores, with the balls and equipment available at the time, seem to me almost miraculous. For example, Harold Hilton scored 305 over Muirfield in 1892, and J. H. Taylor 309 over St Andrews in 1901.

The first Open to be won with a rubber-cored ball, a Haskell, was played at Hoylake in 1902, where Alex Herd scored 307. In the same year Charles Hutchings won the Amateur Championship, also at Hoylake, beating S. H. Fry by one hole in a dramatic finish. His grandson, my friend and neighbour, Geoffrey Hutchings, tells me that Charles, too, played with a Haskell, the first Amateur Champion to do so. From then on winning scores at the Open fell, on average, progressively lower, until a record of 268 was achieved by Tom Watson at Turnberry in 1977.

Tom, however, has numerous advantages, besides better golf balls, over Boskers and me in the days of our youth.

To begin with, his clothes are neat and comfortable, designed for the game, and he wears shoes with spikes in them. We golfed in our 'gallowses'; sometimes we wore boots and sometimes our feet were bare.

He wears a glove on his left hand to ensure a firm hold on grips which themselves are scientifically designed to give maximum purchase. Our hands were bare and liable to slip on shafts usually bound with shiny leather but sometimes naked.

He has a caddy, who hefts an enormous bag – in which, for all I know, he sleeps at night – a bag containing a putter, nine glinting steel-shafted irons and four steel-shafted woods protected by furry hoods, spare golf balls of the finest quality, spare plastic tees of various lengths, spare visors for the sun, a selection of other headgear for wet and windy conditions, feather-light rainwear, an umbrella, a few small towels, a copy of the Rules of Golf, glucose tablets and, quite possibly, a ferret to retrieve balls which disappear down rabbit-holes. We carried our three or four hickory-shafted clubs under our oxters (Scots for 'armpits'). We teed up with pinches of damp sand taken from boxes painted white on the way out and red on the way in. We seldom had any spare balls, and if the one we were playing with went into a rabbit-hole, we scraped and burrowed until we got it out. If the rain came on we had no protection. We simply got wet and endured stoically the subsequent prophetic utterances of our parents concerning pneumonia and inflammation of the lungs.

On the whole, however, I am sure we enjoyed ourselves as much as Tom Watson did at Turnberry. This is the beauty of golf. It is like life, there to be enjoyed in the circumstances in which you find yourself. On the course an impecunious old-age pensioner at Dunaverty has the same pleasure (and pain) as the well-heeled young executive at Sunningdale. And after all, according to legend, the happiest man who ever lived was so poor that he didn't have even a shirt to put on his back. But I suspect his putting was sound. And yip-proof.

There were sad times, of course, when Boskers and I,

failing to negotiate clumps of whin and a burn in spate, had no balls at all to play with. But we had ways of restoring our fortunes.

Occasionally Boskers would wheedle a few old ones from his father, timing his approach to coincide with a parental victory in a monthly medal or a 'bounce' four-ball. Intensive exploration of the course on a Sunday afternoon, when Presbyterian peace descended upon it, often resulted in the discovery of a number of balls in reasonable condition. Once, when investigating a large rabbit-burrow near the 4th hole, I found no fewer than three balls in its dark recesses, one of them an almost new bramble-marked 'Colonel', which turned out to be a 'floater'. With that 'Colonel' in my pocket I felt as a miner in the Yukon must have felt after unearthing a nugget of pure gold.

On other occasions we found ourselves in the joyful position of being able to buy new balls: balls of the highest quality at 9d. each.

In the years between the wars a rifle range used by local Territorials bordered the seaward side of the course, running parallel to the 5th, 6th, 8th and 11th holes. Indeed, the present 5th tee was the firing point at 1000 yards. When the 'Terriers' were practising, a red flag was hoisted on a high bluff above the target area, and golfers avoided the danger- ous holes as far as possible. It was awkward when a rifle shot cracked out during your backswing on a four-foot putt; but you took comfort from the fact that at any moment your opponent was liable to suffer the same traumatic experience. Boskers and I, however, always welcomed a bout of firing on the range.

Behind the target was a high sand-dune, a back-stop for the bullets which went through it. When the firing stopped and the target was lowered and we saw the 'Terriers' marching back toward their hall in the village, we raced to the dune and started digging with feverish hands. We had to be quick, because other lads in the village had the same idea, their state of poverty being equal to, if not worse than ours.

If lucky, we were able to collect a small bagful of lead, which, next time we were in Campbeltown, we sold to

McGinty, the scrap merchant, for amounts ranging from 1s. to 7s.6d. After spending some of the money on ice-cream, at 2d. for well-filled 'wafers' or 6d. for a huge feast of 'banana and ice', we purchased golf balls. These we guarded carefully, changing them for old ones at holes threatened by water or whins; and when their pristine whiteness faded under erratic blows, we restored it with some old paint we discovered in an outhouse at the manse.

The rifle range proved advantageous to others besides Boskers and myself. Every year, in those distant days, there occurred a Visitors versus Locals match; and it was significant, remembering that the date was invariably left to the discretion of the locals, that the deadly conflict nearly always took place on an evening when the range was being used. The locals were used to the intermittent fusillades. The visitors were not, and the effect on their nerves was enough, as a rule, to deprive them of victory.

When we were about sixteen Boskers and I joined the Club, paying an entrance fee of £1 and an annual subscription of 10s. A few years later, to our consternation, the subscription went up to 15s. By then, however, we had both begun to win cash prizes at the local Highland Games – Boskers as a hammer-thrower and ball-putter, myself as a sprinter and jumper – so we were able, at a pinch, to afford it.

At this time we were often joined on the course by my childhood mate, Neil MacLean, the gamekeeper's son, who years before had taught me all I know about the birds and the beasts, wild and tame, which inhabit Southend. At school Neil had played 'rounders' left-handed and could hit a solid rubber ball much farther than anybody else. Now he played golf right-handed and could still, on occasions, hit a golf ball farther than anybody else. He had, of course, a natural eye for a ball-game; but I believe his success as a golfer provided evidence in support of a theory of mine.

I reckon that *coiteachs* ('left-handers') make the best golfers, *playing right-handed*. This would appear to be logical, in view of the fact that an effective golf stroke (by someone playing right-handed) depends largely on the strength of the left arm and hand and the firmness of the left side during the swing and follow through. In his youth Ben Hogan played left-handed. Playing right-handed he became one of the finest strikers of a golf ball who ever lived. And in more modern times there is the case of David Graham. As a youth in Australia he got his handicap down to single figures with a cast-off set of left-handed clubs. At the age of sixteen he began to play right-handed and prospered so well in the game that in 1980 he won the US Open Championship.

My brother Archie was inclined to be left-handed. At cricket, though he bowled right-handed, he batted as a *coiteach*. At golf he used left-handed clubs; but his success as a golfer never equalled his success at other sports: soccer, for example, in which he gained a 'Blue' at Glasgow University. I often wonder if, after World War II, during which he served as an officer with the Argyll and Sutherland Highlanders, I might have succeeded in persuading him to follow Neil MacLean's example and change to 'right-handed' golf. Would he have lowered his handicap to single figures, or even to scratch? The question must remain unanswered. Archie was fatally wounded on the plain of Gerbini in Sicily, in July 1943.

Neil, too, is long dead. But while they lived, both Archie and Neil saw most of their shots flying far and fair. They had no need to worry about the advantages or disadvantages of carbon shafts and high-velocity golf balls. They never reached the age after which, according to Henry Cotton (or Dr Flaherty), you lose two yards off your drive with every passing year.

MEMO

My distance is due more to the strength of my legs than to any power I may be getting from my arms, hands and fingers.

Jack Nicklaus

6. Democracy at Dunaverty

There are many who argue that golf is a democratic game in which aristocrat and artisan, merchant and mechanic, scratch man and 'rabbit' can come together on the fairways as friends and equals. This is true, up to a point, in the same way as it is true that Scotland and England are democratic countries.

Under our present parliamentary systems, in which everybody over the age of eighteen has a vote, a mole-catcher should, in theory, enjoy the same rights and privileges as a prime minister. In practice, however, as mole-catchers and prime ministers constantly remind us, this is not the case. Our society is the most class-ridden in Europe, with the exception, perhaps, of Russia's. So, I am prepared to concede, is golf, both on and off – and particularly off – the course.

In society as a whole it is usually 'lang pedigrees', intellectual achievement and money which provide the barriers between the so-called 'haves' and 'have nots'. In golf it is playing ability, age differentials and sex (in the proper meaning of the word) which are the divisive elements.

The young man who cheerfully slams his way around a municipal course, wearing bicycle clips to protect his trouser-ends on a damp September morning and thinking the while about the cans of beer and ham sandwiches he will share with his buddy in the car park at the end, is a class apart from the white-moustached, ruddy-faced old character who pokes his way around a private course, wearing plus-fours and an old school tie, and thinking of the gin and tonic, roast beef and gingerbread which await him and his foursome partners in the clubhouse.

The steely-eyed scratch man, tartan-trousered, polo-neck-ed, visored against the sun, counting birdies as he goes, is in a class apart from the balding, uncertain, dishevelled Professor of Zoology whose knowledge of birdies is much wider off the course than on. A youth producing golf shots with the suppleness and silent power of a hungry cobra is in a class apart from the septuagenarian whose swinging movements are as 'distinct from harmony divine' as 'the constant creaking of a country sign'.

Female golfers, of course, are in a class apart from all male addicts. And in the precincts of their own sacred temples, the ladies' clubhouses, they plot and plan even more internal divisions, calling them gold, silver and bronze. They are also assiduous in their demands to the male committee that they should be afforded more time on the course and haughtily resistant to the implication in the replies that more time might indeed be given if they paid subscriptions equal to the men's.

There is a facile saying that on a golf course all men (including women) are equal. Contrast this with Francis Bacon's dictum: 'There is little friendship in this world, and least of all between equals.' Discounting the suspicion that Bacon must have composed his sad commentary after having been beaten 'out in the country' by Shakespeare, you will find that these two apparently paradoxical statements, in juxta-position, reveal a golfing secret. This is that on a golf course you discover friendship, simply because there is no equality.

Golfers of varied abilities, ages and sexes recognize the class in which their Creator has ordained they should operate. They do so happily, untouched by rancour.

The 18-handicapper shows no resentment towards a fellow-member who is scratch, because at the back of his mind is always the fond hope that one day, with patience and perseverance, he too will become a scratch man. And the scratch man is always willing to play with an 18-handicapper, giving him a stroke a hole and showing no contempt or distaste for the other's mistakes, because at one time, in the dawn of his wisdom, he also made the same mistakes. (In any case, he knows that, barring miracles, he is going to win the game.)

The young man with the bicycle clips meets in competition with the white-moustached wearer of an old school tie, and they shake hands on the result as fellow addicts and brothers.

At the conclusion of their round the tartan-trousered scratch man shares a convivial dram with the Professor of Zoology and may even express interest in birdies which have legs and wings.

In the clubhouse the youth with the supple swing forgives his geriatric opponent for sinking a ten-yard putt to beat him on the 18th and listens readily to the other's memories of great Walker Cup matches he has witnessed in the past.

When the ladies appear at the Annual Golf Dinner, their brogues, tweed skirts and severely tailored slacks replaced by gorgeous dresses in many colours, their talk is not of divisions, gold, silver and bronze, but of golf in general and, it may be, of the new (male) club champion's handsome appearance.

I believe that a touch of golf, like a touch of nature, makes 'the whole world kin'. This is because all faithful golfers understand that in order to achieve happiness in the game they must accept without enmity or discontent that inequalities are inevitable. This does not mean to say, of course, that they ever give up their search for the holy grail, in the shape of a perfectly executed golf shot.

Boskers and I discovered early that as golfers we were fated to encounter many barriers.

In our youth the Dunaverty Clubhouse was of corrugated iron, about 25 feet long and 15 broad, built in a popular pre-World War I style called Spieresque. Magazines of the period, to which my parents subscribed, including *Chambers's Journal* and *Life and Work*, were filled with advertisements containing illustrations of the various fancy erections – tennis pavilions, church halls and even public loos – which the enterprising firm of Spier was ready to provide with a minimum of delay. I think that Spier must have been among the originators of the 'pre-fab' idea.

The clubhouse built by the firm for Dunaverty had windows so high that it was impossible to see out of them, unless you stood on the plain wooden table positioned carefully in the middle of the concrete floor. The inner walls were lined with lockers, and in a corner behind the door there stood a wash-hand basin. Beneath the lockers, about 18 inches above the floor, there projected a narrow wooden seat which ran round the whole interior, with the exception of the door space. The prevailing smell inside was of damp clothes, leather and pipe tobacco smoke.

One day, soon after we joined the club, Boskers and I essayed an entry. We had no lockers. Lockers cost more money than we could afford and, in any case, as healthy sixteen-year olds, we were perfectly happy to sling clubs on our shoulders as we cycled to and from the course. We were curious, however, to discover what went on within this curious, somehow secretive place.

As we opened the door we saw, sitting on either side of the table on the wooden seat, the four fairly elderly members who had completed their round a minute or two before us and, indeed, had inhibited our ordinarily speedy passage along the last few fairways. We knew them well, of course.

The day was cold, with slight showers from the south-west wisping over the course. All four still had on the ordinary cloth suits and hard collars in which they had been playing. The suits were already steaming a little.

One of the four was the 'schoolmaister', James Inglis Morton, burly and solid, with the bushy blond moustache which contrasted so interestingly with his scant dark hair. Another was 'Dr Jim': James Niven, the parish doctor, a slim, wiry man with a narrow moustache and a bleak, inquiring eye. During our short lives Boskers and I had been attended to by both of them, receiving from one knowledge and discipline and from the other advice on the kind of medicine required to cure our juvenile ills and pains.

A third member was Boskers's father, Captain James Taylor, TD, farmer and former officer with the Argyll and Sutherland Highlanders: a tall, handsome man with a kittle temper not unlike that of my own father. The fourth was Dick Gillon, an itinerant fisherman and rabbit-catcher whose sinuous build and dark complexion may or may not have been handed down by a survivor of the Spanish Armada. Both he and Captain Taylor had been founder members of the club. Indeed, Dick had been employed as one of the first greenkeepers. His engagement, however, had come to an acrimonious end when it was discovered that he was building tees with boulders and rubble concealed only by a thin layer of earth and clubs were 'shattered in shard on shard'.

As Boskers and I went in we noticed at once that mingling with the smell of tobacco-smoke was another aroma, that of what fastidious folk of the period called 'spirits'. There was a sudden opening and shutting of the table drawer and a burst of coughing, accompanied by a shuffling and a rustling of papers on the table. Inimical faces were turned in our direction.

Nobody spoke for a second or two. Then, in the sardonic, intimidating voice for which he was famous, Dick inquired: 'Have ye lost something?'

The atmosphere was chill. Boskers and I mumbled a few inept words. We hesitated, but no intimation of hospitality was conveyed to us.

'Sorry!' I said.

We left smartly, shutting the door behind us.

It was a long time before we collected enough courage to go inside the clubhouse again, even on competition days. We recognized our place in the scheme of things: a lowly place which could only be improved as we grew older and wiser and our golf better.

About two years later I applied for a handicap. To my surprise Mr Morton, who had become the secretary, himself played with me to mark the two cards I needed. The previous suspicious relationship between master and pupil, veteran golfer and raw beginner was gradually smoothed away as, during the games, I absorbed much wisdom concerning golf.

By that time Mr Morton's physical powers were in decline, while my own were burgeoning. Occasionally I outdrove him by fifty yards, but this never worried him. There was no reason why it should worry him, because my pitching and putting were simply no match for his.

At the short 4th, on our first outing, I found my tee-shot in a clump of bent not far from the greenside. As I slashed my way out with more enthusiasm than skill I saw him stroking his big moustache and smiling. 'You remind me of the time James Braid played the course, advising us on the positioning of some of the greens – particularly this one. He was in some bent not far from where you are now. But he got the ball out with one easy swing of his niblick and it landed and stopped inches from the hole.'

That was one lesson I learnt that day, 'easy' being the key-word. Even now, when I remember, the word is magic. Another lesson was provided at the same hole.

The short 4th at Dunaverty is situated in a quiet hollow with tall, grass-covered sand-dunes on three sides. Mr Morton's tee-shot had landed short, and it appeared to me that he would have to play a high pitch over the dune which hid the hole from him. When I saw him addressing the ball with a mid-iron and aiming almost at right angles to the direct line I wondered, in a moment of near-horror, if at last golf had driven him mad. Then his ball streaked through a small gap between the dune in front and the one on the left. It struck half-way along the down-slope of the dune on the left, careered around the dry, close-cut grass on to the steep side of the dune behind the green and finally, like a toboggan on the Cresta Run, sped back and down towards the flag. It came to a stop a yard from the hole. 'Local knowledge,' said Mr Morton, patting my shoulder.

Now that my drive at the 4th has become increasingly short I take a delight, when finding my ball in a similar position, in executing Mr Morton's shot against a youthful opponent and watching his initial expression of anxious surprise change to one of carefully camouflaged chagrin as my ball sweeps around 'the wall of death' and curves in sweetly towards the flag. A good drive may be a 'slosh' and a source of modest pleasure, but so is a cunning use of local knowledge. And herein, I believe, lies one reason why you can remain happy in golf until your Creator decides it is time you gave up your local membership and, having faithfully paid the dues, joined at last the finest of our country clubs beyond the sky.

Mr Morton's kindness in offering to mark my cards for handicap, his advice in word and action and his obvious pleasure in the games we played, then and afterwards, taught me a third lesson, though at the time it was less obvious than the others: the lesson that golf can be a foundation for friendship between the unlikeliest people.

At this point it may be recorded that my first handicap was 18. Many years later I got it down to 5. Now, inexorably, it is rising again like a slow tide. As I write, it is 11. By the time you read this – who knows? The new handicapping system may have engulfed me in a sea of fractions.

James Braid was not the only notable person to play the links of Dunaverty. Over the years our turf has been trodden by professional champions like Sandy Herd, Hector Thomson, Bobby Walker and Eric Brown. Sir Ernest Holderness, ten times an English amateur international, played a round over the course in the 1920s.

Boskers and I, as schoolboys, observed with awe Sir Ernest's majestic drives and accurate pitches. Weeks later we read the article he wrote for a London newspaper in which he referred to 'the quaint course of Dunaverty at the Mull of Kintyre' and to its 'members with their hard hats and clubs tucked underneath their arms'.

He also told the story of what happened on the first tee as he watched an elderly farmer with whiskers and a set of ancient clubs playing across the fairway towards the (then) 3rd hole.

'Who is the dear old gentleman?' he inquired of his caddy.

The caddy sneered and spat. He knew the farmer well as a local character with a notoriously irascible manner and an affectionate nickname. 'That's no' a gentleman!' he laughed. 'That's owld Yadi!'

During the 1928 Walker Cup match at Royal St George's, Sandwich, Sir Ernest was defeated 10 and 8 by G. Voigt. After the public fun he had made of Dunaverty we were disinclined to mourn for him. As true Scots we like to make fun of ourselves but are not so keen on outsiders 'taking the mickey'.

Another guest at Dunaverty was S. L. McKinlay, the cultured journalist who played eleven times for Scotland as an amateur and eventually became editor of the *Glasgow Evening Times*. Sam is a real amateur, with whom it is always a pleasure to play, his iron shots matching in their elegant crispness the stories he is so fond of telling.

One summer afternoon I stood with him on the 16th tee at Dunaverty. The hole measures 144 yards, with destruction on the left in the shape of a sandy gully sloping down towards the river. At the back of the tiny green are clumps of whin. That day the wind was strong from the north, directly against us. I was thinking of using a driver, and it was with interest that I saw Sam take from his bag a 4-iron.

He then executed one of the best golf shots I have ever seen – a powerful 'driller', so powerful indeed that I was sure his ball would run through into the whins. It struck the green about a yard from the flag, but instead of leaping forward, it kicked up and stopped dead.

'How the heck did you do that?' I demanded.

'Simple,' he told me. 'Hands in front of the ball at the address. Swing down slow and nip through.'

Simple? I have tried to do exactly as he told me many times, but the resulting shots have never been as effective – or artistic – as Sam's.

After that visit he made Dunaverty the subject of one of his felicitous weekly articles in the *Glasgow Herald*. Our greens he described as 'boiler plates', and for this unkind observation I had to reprimand him in a letter to the *Herald* pointing out that he had seen our greens after a long dry spell and that Dunaverty had no watering system. (It has now, I hasten to add.) But we remain friends, even though he did reveal in another article that my golf is punctuated with loud exhortations to my ball: 'You hound of hell, keep out of there!'

Thankfully, Dunaverty is no longer pitted by the hoof marks of grazing Clydesdale horses, though because of their departure in favour of tractors from the farms on which it lies, we are now unable to gather succulent mushrooms on the 17th fairway. Being comparatively short, however, and at times inhabited by flocks and herds of sheep and cattle, the course has always lived under the shadow of its famous neighbour, Machrihanish, which, with its length of some 6300 yards, has championship status. Nevertheless, while Machrihanish can boast of Hector Thomson, who won the British Amateur Championship at St Andrews in 1936 and subsequently became a distinguished professional, Dunaverty has a longer list of native champions to its credit.

Heading that list, of course, is Belle Robertson (née McCorkindale), Ladies' British Amateur Champion in 1981, who has a record of international honours unsurpassed by any other woman golfer in Britain.

The daughter of a Southend farmer, Belle went to school with Jock, who will write about her in a subsequent chapter. I am not sure, however, if Jock knows the story of how Belle, as a small girl learning to play golf, amassed a goodly collection of golf balls simply by suggesting to her father, who knew everything about agriculture but nothing about golf, that each time she went to play she required a new one.

Another notable golfer nurtured on our links is J. C. Wilson, runner-up in the Scottish Amateur Championship in 1951 and 1952, who learned to play as a small boy on holiday with his family at Brunerican, my wife's old home. Indeed, Jean remembers, as a teenager, helping to bath the baby who was eventually to play for Scotland six times and for Britain twice in the Walker Cup. It appears, from her description of his loud protests when she lowered him into the soap-suds, that his aversion to water hazards was as acute then as it is now.

Our other VIPs include David Galbraith, champion of Dunaverty during my year as captain in 1957, who later became British Police Champion and still plays a sterling game, and Isobel Crawford (née Wylie), grand-daughter of a Southend blacksmith, who won the Girls' Scottish Championship in 1961 and 1962, reached the semi-final of the Ladies' British Amateur Championship at Newcastle, Co. Down, in 1963 and played for Scotland on several occasions.

Why should a course like Dunaverty, short, unfashionable, hidden among the wilds of the Mull of Kintyre and with a membership of less than 200, tend to produce players of such high calibre?

One reason may be that the narrow fairways, the small greens and the enclosing hazards of sea, river, sand, bracken and whins create an obvious need for accurate hitting. Drives of 300 yards at Dunaverty, deviating only a few feet from 'the straight and narrow', may mean not only the ruination of a card but also the loss of many new balls, either in swelling waters, both fresh and salt, or in thickets of vegetation deep enough to shelter tigers.

Another reason may be that the course, except at the height of summer when visitors to the parish keep the fairways busy, is never crowded and aspiring golfers find ample opportunity to practise. And then there is the condition of the greens, which, though miniature in size and surrounded by electric fences, are, according to an SPGA brochure, 'of the finest quality'.

Belle Robertson and company are our comparatively modern champions. But in the old days, not long after the foundation of the club, there was another individual whose name became legendary.

Jimmy Lyon was a slight, thin-faced Glasgow man with a wispy moustache, who, in his younger days, looked fondly on the wine when it was red. In an effort to accomplish a cure, his family sent him to the small island of Sanda, which lies off the Mull of Kintyre and which, at the time, was inhabited only by a farm-manager and several lighthouse keepers. The nearest pub was two miles away in Southend, across a sometimes choppy sound.

Jimmy stayed with the farmer, who had instructions to keep a close watch on his lodger and encourage him in habits of sobriety. At first the scheme was successful. Jimmy had been a keen golfer, and his first care, on coming to the island, was to cut back acres of heather and bracken and construct a few golf holes and greens on which he could practise. As time went on, and as he played round and round his little course each day, never quite reaching a 19th hole, his health improved and his golf became better than it had ever been. In the outcome he set his heart on crossing to the mainland so that he might take part in the Dunaverty Club's competitions and, as a first step, joined the club by letter.

The farmer, pleased with his lodger's progress, both moral and physical, ultimately agreed to sail him across the sound for a monthly medal and, at the end of the day, Jimmy was announced the winner, with a brilliant score. Dr Niven,

James Taylor and even Dick Gillon had to acknowledge the advent of a bright new star.

On the first outing Jimmy enjoyed a celebration dram but was persuaded by the farmer that they must obey the laws of wind and tide and depart before he took another.

While living on Sanda and helping with lobster creels, Jimmy became an expert boatman, and a time came when he made the suggestion that if he took the boat and crossed to Southend by himself on competition days it would spare the busy farmer a great deal of trouble. His lodger's behaviour having improved so much, the farmer finally agreed.

From then on the Lyon legend began to grow. Three times in four years he was Dunaverty's champion. The drams became more frequent, before and after the competitions. Sometimes he would stay at the Inn for a night or two, partying with friends. Strangely enough, however, the quality of his golf became even more brilliant. So brilliant in fact that the farmer on Sanda was sure that his lodger, in spite of rumours, could never be playing so well except in conditions of comparative sobriety. He was unaware of Jimmy's boast, frequently quoted even today in the Dunaverty clubhouse: 'When I'm sober I can see the hole like a flower-pot. But give me two drams and I can see it like a bucket!'

He often entertained members with exhibitions of his skill, for which he was recompensed by generous quantities of whisky. At will he could play a slice or a pull. He could extricate himself from a bunker with a cleek. Nine times out of ten he could pitch into the centre circle of a ground target 30 yards away. But his most popular trick was to strike a ball teed up on the face of a watch – or as it happened once, on the chin of a fellow member rigid with liquor-based courage.

Members at Machrihanish, hearing of his prowess, issued a challenge to our champion.

Beside the Machrihanish clubhouse there stands a noble structure, the Ugadale Arms, which now, unfortunately, no longer functions as a hotel. If Jimmy could drive a ball over this building, approximately sixty feet high, he would win not only a large sum of money in bets but also unlimited refreshment. The drive, it was stipulated, had to be made from the face of a watch, and the watch must remain undamaged in any way.

The challenge was accepted and a suitable date arranged. A large crowd gathered, including tweed clad members of both Machrihanish and Dunaverty, mufflered miners from the nearby coal-pit, farm workers wearing 'carsekies' and 'bouyangs' and the 'toffs' in evening frocks and dinner-jackets who, before Majorca and the Costa Brava beckoned with fashionable fingers, used to patronize the hotel. (A 'carsekie', by the way, is a blouse of coarse material, usually dark blue and striped with white. 'Bouyangs' are leather thongs tied below the knee to keep up trouser-ends.)

Silence fell as Jimmy took a thick gold 'hunter' watch from his pocket and placed it on the turf about a hundred yards from the frontage of the hotel. On its face he balanced a 'gutty' ball. The story goes that he was drunk at the time, but I simply refuse to believe that, because in the next few seconds, after a few preliminary waggles of his driver, he sent the ball soaring over the hotel, and the watch lay motionless, without even a scratch on its surface.

It may be that the alcohol-filled night that followed was the first substantial setback to Jimmy's 'cure'. In any case, it seems that from about that time his health deteriorated and he was no longer so eager to play golf. Eventually he was taken away from Sanda, and his little course disappeared under the heather and the bracken.

No one can tell me what became of him after his return, sumably to Glasgow. Recently, however, a sad little clue presented itself.

In 1973 Professor Roddy ('Scunnerations of Ezekiel') MacSween was Captain of Dunaverty. One day, looking into the window of an antique shop in Glasgow, he saw a handsome ornament consisting of a ram's horns mounted in silver which bore an inscription indicating that it had been the 'Captain's Prize' to the Dunaverty Champion in 1898. Roddy remembered the list of Captains and Champions hanging on the wall in Southend and particularly one entry.

1898   Captain: D.MacCallum
Champion: J.Lyon

Excited and delighted, therefore, he bought the ornament on the spot, had it cleaned and polished and, a few months later, presented it to the Club as the MacCallum-Lyon Trophy for annual matchplay competition, on handicap.

And so the Lyon legend lives on. But I wonder? Did Jimmy's circumstances, after he left Sanda, become so unhappy that in the end he had to sell – or pawn – his precious prize?

MEMO

Sometimes we are devils to ourselves
When we will tempt the frailty of our powers,
Presuming on their changeful potency.

Shakespeare, Troilus and Cressida

7. Keeping the Faith

In the years leading up to World War II I learned more and more about life and – as a corollary? – more and more about golf. Whether such knowledge made me a better man and a better golfer is a point which must be qualified by one of P.G.Wodehouse's favourite words, namely, 'moot'.

At that time the Rule Book was slimmer than it is now. I was brought up to understand that only in the most unusual circumstances was a golfer relieved of an obligation to 'play the ball where it lies'. For example, a rabbit-scrape was not a rabbit-scrape unless so deep that the top of the ball was beneath the level of the surrounding turf. Loose impediments could only be moved in circumstances so obscure that poor Harry Bradshaw, finding his ball in a bottle carelessly thrown down by a spectator, mistakenly thought he had to play it as it lay, took a 6 and, as a result, lost the 1949 Open Championship. The stymie, which occurred on the putting-green when your opponent's ball lay directly in your line to the hole, was a constant threat to a keen golfer's blood pressure, though, on the other hand, it provided a valuable test of nerve and equally valuable practice in the art of lofting the ball over undesirable obstructions.

Until it was abolished soon after World War II the stymie was an integral part of golf, as far as matchplay was concerned. It added to the adventurous and unexpected flavour of the game and often provided a face-saving alibi for competitors beaten by opponents with higher handicaps.

I am not one of those who screamed for its abolition, despite the fact that on a certain occasion John Cameron laid me one on the 18th green, thus preventing me from winning a matchplay final at Dunaverty. If golf be a sporting mirror of life, which, I confess, is my firm belief, then the stymie ought to be part of it, if only as another tempering process in the steely structure of character.

A hundred years ago Andrew Lang wrote a poem which reflects this view:

> The thing they ca' the stymie o't
>   I find it ilka where!
> Ye 'maist lie deid – an unco shot –
>   Anither's ba' is there!
> Ye canna win intil the hole
>   However gleg ye be,
> And aye, where'er ma ba' may roll,
>   Some limmer stymies me!
>
> I lo'ed a lass, a bonny lass,
>   Her lips an' locks were reid;
> Intil her heart I couldna pass:
>   Anither man lay deid!
> He cam' atween me an' her heart,
>   I turned wi' tearfu' e'e;
> I couldna loft him, I maun part,
>   The limmer stymied me!
>
> I socht a kirk, a bonny kirk,
>   Wi' teind an' glebe an' a';
> A bonny yaird to feed a stirk,
>   An' links to ca' the ba'!
> Anither lad he cam' an' fleeched –
>   *A convairtit U.P.* –
> An' a' in vain ma best I preached,
>   That limmer stymied me!
>
> It's aye the same in life an' gowf;
>   I'm stymied late an' ear';
> This world is but a weary howf,
>   I'd fain be itherwhere.
> But when auld deith wad hole ma corp,
>   As sure as deith ye'll see
> Some coof has played the moudiewarp,
>   Rin in, an' stymied me!

For those unacquainted with the braid Scots tongue let me offer a few 'translations'. *Gleg*, clever. *Limmer*, rascal. *Teind*, stipend. *Stirk*, young cattle beast. *Fleeched*, pled. *Ca'*, drive. *U.P.*, member of the United Presbyterian Church, which, having broken away from it on the principle of patronage, was held in low esteem by the Kirk of Scotland. *Howf*, place. *Coof*, fool. *Moudiewarp*, mole.

The stymie may have been unfair, but then so are certain untended bunkers and the sandy knolls which kick your ball into them. And is it not common for a golfer to find himself stymied by a tree classed as 'listed' and sacred, therefore, to all except the unfortunate player whose ball has bounced behind it off a fallen acorn?

'Golf,' said Jack Nicklaus, 'is not and never has been a fair game.' And no matter how many rules and regulations are made in an attempt to change the situation, so it will remain. Where would the excitement be, in life or golf, without the factor of luck?

My most influential mentors in the ethics and rules of golf were John Cameron, the salmon-fisher who became a farmer – and who beat me at the 19th in that matchplay final – and Jim Greenlees, the local postman. They are gone now, but in their day they played golf well enough to take part in the *Evening Times* Foursomes and, on one occasion, to reach the quarter-finals. Both also became club captains and both won the club championship several times. Complete integrity was the name of their game, and they made it their business to ensure that it was the name of mine, too.

Those were the days, of course, before administrators of the welfare state – inadvertently, I am sure – inclined us to believe that 'take' is a better word than 'give'. Self-discipline was not a reactionary word, and consideration for your fellow men was not reckoned to be a sign of weakness. I learned that in order to enjoy golf to the full you must show respect and consideration for your partners and opponents and suppress any temptation to cheat either them or, even more important-ly, yourself.

John was persuasive in his teaching, guiding a raw youth by example and an occasional word of explanation. Jim was a harder man and peremptory in pointing out faults: no doubt thirty years' experience as club treasurer had an influence in this regard. Many a time I enjoy a memory of his slightly querulous voice: 'Stand still and silent when your partner or opponent is playing a shot. Never stand behind him on the tee, except when the sun is in his eyes and you are helping him to follow the flight of his ball. When he is putting never stand near or behind the hole in his direct line. If you are asked to hold the flag do so at arm's length, standing at right angles to his line of putt, at the same time making sure that your shadow does not fall across his line. Never fail to replace a divot. And for heaven's sake throw any litter you may have into the tee boxes.'

In later years, when we played together with understanding, I used to say to them: 'By praising my youthful strength and skill you have just conned me into taking a 5-iron for a shot which needed a 4-wood at least. What about your ethics now – all the courtesy and consideration you taught me to show to partners and opponents?' (I have paraphrased my actual words, which, as you probably suspect, were stronger and more basic.)

Jim would chuckle in a sardonic way and point out that nobody had suggested that I should use a 5-iron: it was my own decision. John would take up his customary open stance, hit a glorious spoon shot – 'bringing it in from leeward' in his seaman's language – and smile his guileless smile. 'Gamesmanship,' he would say, 'is another story. Don't you think it makes a friendly game all the more enjoyable?'

And of course it does, when blossoming in the ground of good fellowship.

At school and university it was often suggested to us that golf was not a team game, like football and cricket for example, and therefore of inferior value as a character-building exercise. John and Jim made me realize that it is perhaps the most splendid team game of all and a character-builder of the subtlest and most powerful order. The team for which you are playing consists of club golfers and professionals all over the world. If you fail to count a stroke or disobey a rule you are cheating them all and letting the whole side down. By keeping strictly to the fairway of golfing ethics you are helping in a small way to uphold not only the honour of the game but also the broad human ideal of 'love your neighbour'.

Because there is no referee or umpire to overlook your every action on the course, ethical decisions are entirely your own responsibility. When you come to think of it, is this not a far more daunting test of character than any to be experienced in an ordinary team game?

Of course, the crux of the matter is that while playing golf you are never alone. Your Creator is there, his watchful eye on everything you do, even in the deep, almost impenetrable woods. And your character is built upon how you react to this situation.

He may smile with pleasure when you decide to be honest, but His testing seldom stops at this point. No immediate reward of a booming drive or a crisp iron shot may be offered. Instead, He may continue to burden you with snap hooks from the tee, shanks along the fairway and sclaffy approaches. Or even – because as far as golf is concerned, your Creator has a definite sense of humour – with bizarre accidents like that which overtook a San Francisco golfer not long ago. His ball lay on the grassy overhang of a bunker on the greenside. As he shaped up to play a simple chip, congratulating himself on having avoided the sandy hazard, he sneezed. His false teeth flew out, fell upon the ball and knocked it back into the bunker.

But at the end of the day your Creator generally sees to it that the golfer experiences a glow of satisfaction – enhanced, perhaps, by a gin and tonic and companionable conversation in the club bar – in having kept the faith with millions of team-mates of every creed and colour. And tomorrow is another day and another game, and you can mingle with your companions on the golf course in a spirit of rectitude.

Professionals in other sports are sometimes tempted to cheat and manipulate the rules when they reckon the referee or the umpire is not looking. This may be one cause of the hooliganism which, in recent years, has become so dangerous a sore on the sporting body. But only on the rarest of occasions does a golfer attempt to cheat even when thousands of pounds or dollars or yen hang upon his decision and when there is every chance of his getting away with it. In almost every big tournament there is at least one instance of a frustrated but honest golfer informing his partner that while addressing his ball in some secluded glade it happened to move and that, therefore, he had incurred a penalty.

One of the most impressive examples of golfing integrity I have ever seen was provided by John Panton. Searching for his ball in a patch of rough, in the first round of an important Scottish tournament, he thought he had found it, a new No 4 Dunlop. As he prepared to address it, however, his caddie found another ball nearby, also a new No 4 Dunlop. Unable to say for certain which was his, John played the first one but imposed a penalty on himself for having played the wrong ball!

Panton, of course, had previously earned his sobriquet of 'Honest John' at the Open at St Andrews in 1946. One evening, while innocently practising putting on a green on the New Course, he realized that the New was one of the qualifying courses and that by playing on it he had broken a rule of stroke play. He immediately reported his inadvertence to the Royal and Ancient and was disqualified.

Among spectators at golf tournaments there is no hooliganism, no obscene shouting. When Tom Watson or Jack Nicklaus or Tony Jacklin stands on the last green addressing a putt for the Open there is not a sound among those looking on. Gulls may be heard mewing on a distant shore, the drone of a faraway plane may echo faintly in the sky, a gentle wind may rustle among the marquees and tents, but around the green even the grass forgets to whisper. The ethics of the game require silence when a golfer is preparing to play a shot and thousands of faithful spectators are as one in providing it.

When the putt goes in and lusty cheers ring out to relieve the tension, the loser refrains from kicking or spitting at his opponent. Instead, he smiles and pats the champion on the back, and you feel proud that you are a golfer.

Another pleasant aspect of the game is that its rules regarding amateurism and professionalism are so nicely balanced that they remain almost unnoticeable. You are a professional if your main occupation is playing or teaching golf. You are an amateur if your main occupation is something else. It is as simple as that.

If, in athletics, Alan Wells wishes to retain his amateur status he cannot compete against a professional runner. In Rugby Union, several star players have had to retire from active participation after writing books on the subject and thereby becoming 'professionals'. In golf, Jock and I can write about the game to our hearts' content and play 'bounce' matches with such as John Panton, Eric Brown, Bernard Gallacher and Sam Torrance and still be classed as amateurs. They are human beings. We are human beings. They are our friends, and the only thing that matters is that we all love golf and play the game according to our conscience.

If Jock and I were good enough we could play in the Open and tie for the championship, as Roger Wethered did at St Andrews in 1921, or even win it as Bobby Jones did no less than three times – at Royal Lytham and St Annes in 1926, at St Andrews in 1927 and at Hoylake in 1930. No professional would object, no other amateur would object. Only the quality of our golf would be of the slightest interest to other golfers. In golf the game is the thing, and snobbish considerations concerning social status – whatever that may mean – simply do not exist. If such a condition as social status did exist on the golf course its measure would be your handicap.

Would to God, as the old Romans used to say, that the governments of this world were chosen on the basis of a golfing meritocracy. With Arnold Palmer as president of the United States, Roberto de Vicenzo in charge of Argentina, Gary Player guiding South Africa, Bernhard Langer a supremo in Europe, Bob Charles lording it in New Zealand and Peter Thomson in Australia, with Neil Coles as prime minister of Great Britain, Keith MacKenzie, formerly secretary of the Royal and Ancient, as chancellor of the exchequer and Bernard Gallacher as secretary of state for Scotland, what a wonderfully peaceful world we would live in. Hogan's principles would replace those of Friedman. Summit conferences would concern the size and quality of golf balls (and the brotherhood of man) rather than the size and quality of nuclear missiles (and destruction and death). Books on golf would become more influential than those penned by Marx or Hitler. Peter Alliss, to popular acclaim, would be given a share of radio and television time much larger than that given to Michael Parkinson and Sir Robin Day put together. And perhaps more neighbours would learn to love more neighbours and the doctrines of jealousy, hatred and violence would vanish from the earth.

MEMO

There is but one law for all, namely, that law which governs all law, the law of our Creator, the law of humanity, justice, equity – the law of nature, and of nations.

Edmund Burke

8. 'Hit the Bloody Ball!'

In the early 1930s, after leaving Glasgow University, I was intently engaged upon learning the craft of writing, first as a reporter on the *Campbeltown Courier*, where I was also office boy, occasional printer and assistant editor, then as a reasonably successful freelance author. I was also courting Jean McKerral, the little girl whom I had met years before at the dancing class. (At this point it must be made clear that my desire to marry Jean had nothing at all to do with the fact that the greater part of the Dunaverty golf course lay within the bounds of her father's farm and that because of this she was allowed free membership of the club.) But in spite of those other exciting and enjoyable and time-consuming activities I remained a faithful golfer.

The imminence of marriage and, in preparation for it, the building of a bungalow on the Machribeg shore – only the distance of a drive and a pitch from the course – did not, to any great extent, reduce the number of games I played. Indeed, on the evening of 23 June 1936, old Sammy Mitchell and I played in the final of the Amod-McNeil Quaich (our unofficial foursomes championship) and won it. The next day, 24 June, Jean and I were married in Southend Parish Church by the Rev. Kenneth MacLeod and the Padre.

My mother was inclined to criticize this apparent lack of sensitivity on the part of her eldest son; but when I pointed out that the Marquis of Montrose had played golf on the day before his wedding and that as a good Tory and admirer of the aristocracy she should be more magnanimous in her judgement, she forgave me a little. My father made no comment, being more concerned, as he said himself, with 'getting his bowels right for the big day'.

Jean's father and mother, by this time, were both dead. She herself, however, was full of understanding. The final had to be played by 30 June, a date which would occur in the midst of our honeymoon, and it was better that I should get the game out of the way before rather than during it. Indeed, among the many blessings Jean has brought me is her unfailing patience with my golfing proclivities. When I tell her how much I appreciate this, she makes a calm comment: 'It keeps you out of the pubs, doesn't it?' And, of course, until a slipped disc in 1953 caused her to give up regular play, she was a faithful golfer, too.

We had a fortnight's honeymoon, motoring around Scotland in a sports car loaned to us by a neighbour, young Tom Parsons of Carskiey. Tom himself did not play golf, but his brother Luke was an addict and one of my favourite partners – he still is, though living now in Kent – and Luke, I am certain, did nothing to discourage his brother from making such a kindly gesture to an impecunious golfer. Thanks in part to the temporary possession of the car, the honeymoon, I remember, cost no more than £30, which included, on most nights, our hotel bills.

During that fortnight we did not visit a course or strike a ball. 'Such present joy therein we found/That it exceeded other bliss.' On the first evening after returning to our new home, however, we went across to the golf course and the long battle to remodel Jean's swing was renewed.

Jean's trouble was that as she addressed the ball she held the head of her driver turned in, or hooded. The resultant shot seldom rose more than three feet above the ground and, as a rule, dived left, about fifty yards from the tee, into thick rough or even whins. Why she possessed such an unfortunate habit I cannot imagine, because she could putt like a dream – far better than her husband, in fact.

For years I laboured to correct the fault. Time after time, following my patient advice, she would lay the club head squarely and comfortably behind the ball. Then, as she commenced her backswing, inwards it would twist again – and, *thump*, another quick dive and scuttle would occur. The astonishing thing was that on each occasion she would laugh out loud as if she were perfectly happy. Of course, there may have been a psychological reason for it all. Never in her life has Jean done anything I have told her, and the persistent hooking of her drive may have been an instinctive reaction to my demands, civil and gentle though they normally were. In any case, she said it did not worry her in the least that her drives were unlike those of Joyce Wethered. She enjoyed playing golf, well or badly, and I had better look to my own faults, if I wanted to enjoy it, too.

Her reference to Joyce Wethered indicated the direction of our golfing studies during this inter-war period. Our main course of instruction was a book written by her and her brother Roger, published in 1922, called *Golf from Both Sides*.

A gem of a book, well written in the discursive style of the times, its instructional passages were agreeably free of dogma. When Jean and I used to argue about the way she held her driver she would quote Joyce Wethered on the subject: 'I can see no reason why ladies should not have a free choice in the matter of gripping the club . . . There is no need for women to be afraid of thinking for themselves as to the type of golf they shall play or what implements they shall use in the art of striking the ball. But the nearer the style of women's play approximates to the models set by men, the better it will be for their game in the long run.'

This was advanced thinking in an era when women – even at first the author herself – pit-patted their way around a golf course, wearing heavy, ankle-length skirts, knitted cardigans and bulky felt hats. But after Joyce Wethered (later Lady Heathcote-Amory) had won the British Ladies' Championship four times – in 1922, 1924, 1925 and 1929 – and played against the Americans in the Curtis Cup of 1932, it had become evident to most of her female compatriots that she had 'got it right', as the modern saying goes.

Today, in golf, the equality of the sexes has reached such a condition that veterans like myself – admittedly with failing eyesight – are hard put to it to decide whether the trousered or jeans-encased figure expertly pitching over a bunker two greens away is male or female. Fortunately most of us still retain enough of our faculties to spot the difference on closer inspection, and as often as possible we take steps to avoid playing against young Amazons who can slam the ball fifty yards past us from the tee.

My friend Cecil Middleton tells the story of how, in his youth, he played Joyce Wethered in a match between Oxford University and a team of ladies. Previously, being a proud Yorkshireman, he had sworn in public that if ever he was beaten by a lady he would promptly give up the game. (No male golfer today, however chauvinistic, would dream of making so rash and dangerous a promise.) When he discovered that his opponent in the singles was to be the Ladies' Champion I have no doubt he prayed for divine assistance; and, indeed, according to his story, such assistance was forthcoming. The course chosen for the contest was Little Aston, made difficult and heavy by spring rains. This gave Cecil an advantage, because, with no run on the course, his long carrying shots would always outdistance a woman's. 'I was able to beat her,' he says, 'but had the match been played on a fast seaside course, where her shots would have got plenty of run, I might now have been playing croquet at the Hurlingham Club rather than golf here at Dunaverty.'

In the context of such matches between men and women Joyce Wethered wrote:

The one thing that does count against the ladies on a course such as *Little Aston* is that strength tells very considerably in playing the long iron shots to the green. This is not a typically lady-like shot, in the sense that a lady rarely excels in the art of hard hitting. The effect is rather devastating when a man plumps the ball with his irons from a long distance on to the green with the least apparent difficulty. That must, from necessity and admiration, be suffered gladly, in the hope that some day even a feeble imitation might come within one's scope. In the meantime, the only thing for the ladies to do is to steadily improve the standard of their game, chiefly by concentrating on the best models of iron play . . . and to make the men fight hard to escape the day of retribution.

Sandy Herd was right when he called Joyce Wethered 'a bonny fechter'.

'Angus, ye've nae sweevil at a'!'

Dunaverty: the 4th Green. Southend village is in the background. Can you spot 'the Sleeping Lady'?

Founder-members of Dunaverty Golf Club

'Lost a ball, Sir?' A friendly
spectator at Dunaverty

The Clubhouse, Dunaverty, *c.* 1910

Dunaverty's notorious 17th (as it was fifty years ago, and as it still is today).
Putting: Archie Cameron. Looking on: Alexander Banks, Angus's old
English master

Not a day for golf. Angus discusses the forking of the 6th Green at Dunaverty with Willie MacMillan, greenkeeper

Three generations of writers and golfers. (From right to left): Jock, the Padre, Angus. Status as golfers (in same order): good, bad and indifferent

Another piece of advice for ladies in *Golf from Both Sides* was that they should learn to concentrate more on the game and less on idle chit-chat. And, indeed, Joyce Wethered practised what she preached, as a well-known story illustrates. While putting on the 16th green at St Andrews, during a competition, a goods train rattled by on the now disused line from Leuchars. Steam hissed, a whistle blew and the engine-driver shouted a greeting from a distance of less than twenty yards. The putt went in. Her partner said: 'I thought the train might have put you off.' Said Joyce: 'What train?'

Her brother Roger was also prodigal with sensible advice. Unimpressed by fads and fashions in the way golf was beginning to be taught, he wrote: 'The body should not move back with the club in the backswing. The head should remain in much the same relation to the ball throughout the stroke. Do not fall back upon the right leg at the finish of the swing. Let the arms fly out after the ball with all the abandon of which you are capable.' In other words, echoing Andra Kirkaldy, '*Hit* the bloody ball!'

I reckon that in those few practical words Wethered said all anybody needs to know about striking a golf ball, except one thing: 'Keep your eye on the back of the ball.' And I like the devil-may-care touch in his closing exhortation, indicated by the use of the word 'abandon'. Here is the sign of the champion. Wethered had it. All the more modern 'golfing greats' have it, with Severiano Ballesteros the most spectacular examplar.

There are some who would argue that men like Bobby Jones and Ben Hogan were so well disciplined in their play that 'abandon' was a concept unknown to them. But what about the shot played by Jones at Royal Lytham and St Anne's during the Open Championship of 1926?

At the 16th hole in the final round he had drawn level with his partner, Al Watrous, who, until then, had been leading the field. At the ·17th he drove into a sandy lie in broken ground. Watrous hit his tee-shot straight and true and, using a mid-iron, reached the green with his second. For Jones it was a moment of truth. If he attempted a long shot to the flag the chances were fifty-fifty that he would duff it and find himself in worse trouble, thereby 'blowing' the championship. If he played carefully out of the sand on to the fairway, he might still reach the green in three and sink the putt to remain level with his opponent. On the other hand, if he risked the long shot and it came off, the unexpectedness of it might unsettle Watrous and give him, Jones, an advantage at the next and final hole.

'Ach, to hell with it!' said Jones to himself, or gentlemanly American words to that effect.

He took what was then called a mashie-iron, the equivalent of a modern 4-iron, struck the ball 'with all the abandon of which he was capable' and saw it soar on to the green.

He got his 4. Unnerved, Watrous three-putted and, by doing so, presented Jones with his first victory in the Open.

And what about the shot that Jean and Jock and I saw Ben Hogan play at the 5th hole in the final round of the 1953 Open at Carnoustie?

His second to the sloping green had rolled back almost into a bunker. The ball was in a sandy lie, 50 feet from the pin. He could play it out sideways and safely, with a chance of holing a long putt for his par. Or he could try a pitch straight for the hole, which, if unsuccessful, might cost him a stroke at least. He did not seem to hesitate. That day he was shivering with 'flu, his back was stiff and painful – a legacy of the horrific accident which had almost put an end to his career in 1949 – and yet, with what I think was a 7-iron, he abandoned the easy option and played the most difficult shot in golf, a short pitch off sandy turf. It was so perfectly executed that the ball ran down the green and straight into the hole for a birdie. A new Open Champion was on his way.

Roger Wethered, winner of the British Amateur Championship in 1923, might have won the Open, too; but, like Harry Bradshaw in a year to come, he suffered a cruel variant of those 'rubs of the green' which make golf so exasperating and so exciting.

In the third round of the Open at St Andrews in 1921 he walked forward at the 15th hole to study the line of his second shot. As he stepped backwards, his eye still on the ground formation which would guide him to the green, he trod on his ball, thus incurring a one-stroke penalty. Without it he would have been champion, because at the end of that third day he found himself tied for the trophy with Jock Hutchison, the exiled Scot from Glenview, Chicago. On the Saturday, almost inevitably, he lost the play-off over 36 holes.

The quality of his golf, therefore, makes his comments on the game all the more valuable. In essence, his opinion – and that of his sister – was that if a few fundamental principles were observed in relation to stance and grip, each individual, having his or her own physical and mental characteristics, should be allowed to develop his golf in as natural a way as possible and be wary of becoming 'fouled up in the mechanics of the game', as Babe Zaharias once put it.

Ken Adwick, a modern master, says much the same thing in a different way: 'There is no need to worry about making bodily movements, because if the clubhead path is correct and dominant, then all the complicated movements in the swing are a chain reaction to that thought. Such things as weight transference, pulling down from the top with the left hand, right elbow into the side and so forth – those things will happen anyway.'

I used to be a keen student of every instructional book on golf that was published, and it may be that for a time I became a victim of the disease described by the legendary Ernest Jones (domiciled in America but born in Manchester in 1887) as 'paralysis by analysis'. But then, in 1937, on 23 April, Shakespeare's birthday, Jock was born. Two years later I was stricken with a bout of amoebic dysentery and the year after that I went off to play at being a soldier with millions of others. And when the war ended I had to re-establish my career as a writer and put my mind to becoming a responsible husband and father. There was little time for playing golf and less for studying theory. For a year or two, when Jock was still an infant, I simply 'hit the bloody ball' and found that my handicap remained steady.

Joyce Wethered said that when she hit a good shot she was always aware of the weight of the clubhead throughout the swing, from takeaway to follow-through. When I was able to calm my somewhat desperate temperament, I could get this feeling. When I did, I hit the kind of shots which made me – and still make me – eager for the next round.

MEMO

Sam [Snead] don't know a damn thing about hitting a golf ball, but he does it better than anyone else.

Ben Hogan

9. The Vision Splendid

The *fata morgana*, the mirage of a fairy city on the far horizon, is known to everyone, at any rate in a metaphorical sense. It is well known to golfers, though each golfer, of course, sees in his mind's eye a vision appropriate to his own existence.

> The lunatic, the lover and the golfer
> Are of imagination all compact:
> One sees more devils than vast hell can hold,
> That is, the madman; the lover, all as frantic,
> Sees Helen's beauty in a brow of Egypt;
> The golfer's eye, in a fine frenzy rolling,
> Doth glance from heaven to earth, from earth to heaven;
> And, as imagination bodies forth
> The forms of things unknown, the golfer's brain
> Turns them to shapes, and gives to airy nothing
> A local habitation and a name.

This quotation from *A Midsummer Night's Dream* (with only four words altered) seems to me highly appropriate in the context. I hope the shade of Shakespeare will not only forgive me for abusing it but also spare a twinkle from those lustrous, understanding eyes.

The beauty of a golfer's *fata morgana*, in contrast to the physical kind dependent upon refraction in certain atmospheric conditions, is that it can be summoned up by an effort of imagination, no matter the circumstances in which he finds himself. Indeed, the more unpleasant the circumstances, the more vivid his *fata morgana* can become. Over the years I have found such visions to be powerful therapy for uneasiness in both mind and body.

Jock tells me that the vision which helps him most in times of stress is one in which he stands on the steps of the Turnberry Hotel looking down upon the green and faded yellow expanse of the Ailsa course, with the Firth of Clyde beyond it glinting blue and with Ailsa Craig and Kintyre forming a background of secret romance. In the morning sun the greens glisten with dew and a scent of newly-cut grass floats up to him. In his muscles the desire to swing and strike burgeons like a benign fever.

My own *fata morgana* is similar, though it cannot, of course, match in style that of a member of the elite Association of Golf Writers, who spends his time hobnobbing with the Nicklauses and the Watsons of this world in luxurious haunts like the Turnberry Hotel.

It is a morning in autumn at the Mull of Kintyre. To the north the distant peak of Cnoc Moy is purple with heather. To the west, across the North Channel – *Struithe na Maoile* in the Gaelic – the round hills of Antrim are of a cloudy blue. To the south the Firth of Clyde sparkles in the sun, with Sanda and Sheep Island like lumpy monsters on its surface. To the east the breakfast smoke in the village is dying away, leaving the air fresh and clear, though sometimes this freshness is vitiated by the smell of seaweed rotting on the shore and of dung dropped by the massive Ayrshire cattle which graze the course. Such odoriferous details, however, make no difference to my delight in the vision. In a way they enhance it, as salt does the taste of porridge – if you will pardon, in the context, a culinary comparison.

I am on the first tee at Dunaverty, swinging the stiffness out of my joints before beginning a stern four-ball. As a rule, Jock is in the company, along with such as Boskers and Jim McPhee, Big Allan and Sheriff Donald, Professor Roddy and Dr David, Jackie Wareham and Johnny Trapp, Robertson Finlayson and Jack Milligan, Big Cecil and Gordon Campbell. (Big Cecil gives our game a touch of class. He is a member of the Oxford and Cambridge Golfing Society and still, at over seventy, retains a handicap of 6. Invariably Gordon Campbell, who is a chemist, plays in his kilt. Indeed, as insurance against inclement weather, he carries a spare one in his bag. He never shirks taking part in mixed foursomes, even with the wind gusting to gale force. As a result, the ladies of Dunaverty have all learnt the secret of what a Scotsman wears under his kilt.)

Straight down the middle goes my drive, giving me the chance of an easy 5-iron to the first green, 318 yards away. My 5-iron is, of course, perfect, landing with skilfully applied braking-power a few feet from the pin. To universal acclaim I hole the putt and make a birdie. All is fair in a world that is fair and beautiful; and in the afternoon I will feel healthily relaxed and my daily thousand words will come streaming out like diamonds from Aladdin's satchel.

Such stuff are visions made of.

They come to me now when golf games are precluded by 'flu or by spasms of rheumatism in my right hip. They came to me once when for a month my right hand was wrapped in painful bandages having been smashed by a windowful of heavy double-glazing. And they came to me during World War II as I lay in slit trenches or tried to sleep in an open field with the future Field-Marshal Sir Bernard Law Montgomery's guns 'knocking them for six' only a few hundred yards away. For a few minutes they wrought therapy on disordered bodily and mental functions and helped to buttress the will to endure unpleasantness.

And always, thus far in my life, the vision has eventually taken solid form and shape. I stand on the first tee, swinging at the daisies, with my friends around me, and I thank my Creator for having cured my ills, for having provided politicians of the extreme right and the extreme left with a few sharp lessons and for having made me a faithful golfer. It matters little that the vision is seldom complete and that more often than not the rain is riding in a snell wind from the sou'-west, that the sea is hurtling up against Dunaverty Rock and the burn a brown torrent, that my opening drive consists of a feeble trickle into the rough immediately in front of the tee and that my companions make unsympathetic comments about my putting. The important thing is, I am golfing again, and life, on the whole, is good.

It has been my experience that a temporary lay-off tends to

improve the quality of your golf, at least for a time. In the first round I played after the accident to my hand I scored level 4s, which made the pain I had suffered well worth while. Did this happen because I was more relaxed and happy or because I held the clubs more gingerly than usual and was unable, therefore, to reproduce the wild hammer-throwing swings which frequently mar my golf?

Henry Longhurst used to tell of an occasion when he asked Bobby Locke for some advice about putting. Locke's immediate response was that the putter should be held very loosely. 'Ha,' said Longhurst, 'but what about when you have a four-footer to tie for the Open?' Said Locke: 'Hold it looser still!'

During World War II I was starved of golf for six years, though, of course, I played rounds in my imagination many times. Everywhere we went I looked for golf courses; but none appeared on our devious paths through Madagascar, India, Persia, Sicily and Italy, Belgium and Germany. Once, during a short interlude in the Middle East, we did come upon a course in Cairo, belonging, I believe, to the Gezira Sporting Club, which I played with borrowed clubs. As we struck drives off matting tees, iron shots from flat scrub and putts on 'greens' consisting mainly of sand and some kind of bituminous substance, and as the dry and dusty smells of Egypt invaded our nostrils, I offered a grateful prayer to my Creator for having decided that my home course should be Dunaverty. Though sometimes whipped by wind and deluged by rain it remains green and lush and rewards members with the scent of wild thyme on the fairways around the turn, and its greens run smooth and true.

The strange thing is, on the bumpy, sandy greens of Cairo, I putted much better than ever I have done at Dunaverty.

When the war in Europe ended we waited patiently for our demobilization papers to come through. At the time my men and I were billeted in a disused cement factory at Hardegsen in Germany, with plenty of time to play golf had we been given the chance. But nobody in the higher echelons of command appeared to be interested in golf. Cricket and soccer were our official recreational activities – though, of course, a number of my adventurous Fusiliers found other private and unofficial ones – and I spent my time trying to persuade good cricketers and footballers in other companies to seek transfers to the MT section.

We did win the Brigade soccer championship, thanks in part to the brilliant goalkeeping of the appropriately named Fusilier Gold, who drove the water-truck and was six foot six tall. We also played cricket against the Green Howards on a pitch in Bonn. During the match the MTO distinguished himself – or rather, extinguished himself – by being bowled out twice for a duck by a Yorkshire county player whose deliveries, to a gentle Scot at any rate, resembled the 'all-dreaded thunderstone'.

Then one day, to my astonishment and pleasure, news came through that a golf tournament had been arranged for the British Army, to be played in Denmark. I am not certain that we ever knew the name of the course. Enough for us that it offered a few days' leave, a taste of civilized living after the recent brutish activities, and a temporary escape from the boredom of peace in a strange country.

There was, however, one awkward condition. Entries were confined to those with handicaps of 5 and under. But to officers and men who had become accustomed to dodging shells and bullets in convenient fox-holes, juggling with spare parts 'indents' to the RASC and fictionalizing NAAFI returns (especially in regard to beer and whisky) this did not present too serious a problem, either moral or material. In a distant civilian era Charlie Cope's handicap had been 7 and mine 8. We put our heads together and decided that had Hitler allowed us to continue to improve our golf during the previous six years we should, without doubt, have got them down to 5 – perhaps, indeed, to scratch. But we made a concession to honesty and sent in our entry forms, both as 5-handicap golfers.

The officers' mess in Hardegsen was in a large house which had obviously belonged to somebody of sophisticated tastes in both cheese and wine. At every evening meal quivering rounds of Camembert were unveiled: rounds which, when pierced, emitted a stench far more daunting (to me) than that of the rotting seaweed and the dung at Dunaverty. The taste I found to be supportable, however, when tempered by draughts of a beautiful red German wine taken daily from the cellar. (I cannot remember the full and proper name of that wine. Would a connoisseur find a clue in part of it which floats in my memory: the word 'Ruppertsberger'?)

It was over the cheese and wine one evening that Charlie and I announced our impending holiday in Denmark, and great was the chagrin and jealousy displayed by all the non-golfers. According to them we had been a .pair of 'skivers' during hostilities – not even a tiny wound between us – and now, in time of peace, we had reached the very depths of 'skivery'. But the CO had played golf, though to a handicap so generous that had he declared it as 5 his skulduggery would have become immediately apparent on the course. He gave us his blessing and a short dissertation on the art of putting – in which he claimed to be an expert – and finally a grim warning that if we let the Royal Scots Fusiliers down, on or off the fairways, we might find ourselves dismissed from the Army, with ignominy. (Such a threat of course, even had it been serious, would have had no effect on us whatsoever. Now that Hitler was *kaput* our main ambition was to be dismissed from the Army, under any conditions, as soon as possible.)

Charlie and I found some old clubs and balls in the cement factory and began serious practice. Gradually our swings took shape as we put behind us the idea of grenade throwing. A week before we were due to leave for Denmark our confidence was high.

Then the blow fell. A message came through that certain conditions in the tournament were being hastily revised and that only golfers with handicaps of scratch would be allowed to play. It was revealed that a thousand golfers had been thinking along the same lines as Charlie and myself and had declared handicaps of 5. And that another thousand had gone even farther along the road of fantasy by claiming marks of 4 and 3 and 2 and 1.

Charlie and I said goodbye to our holiday and went back to the Camembert and the Riesling and the ribald comments of our fellow officers. The CO said that our faces made him laugh 'like a drain' – a common simile in the Army and an irritating one, especially when you are ignorant of what kind of stinking watercourse is being referred to. I have been told that a 'drain' is a bird, but the name is to be found in no dictionary possessed by me. And if all this has an edge of surliness, it is exactly how Charlie and I felt at the time.

Soon afterwards, however, we were demobbed and returned happily to our wives and families. And then, one fine day, we stood again on the first tees of our respective courses and flexed strong, if rusty muscles. It was our turn to 'laugh like drains', in sheer ecstasy, as our fairy cities in the sky became reality.

MEMO

Golf is deceptively simple, endlessly complicated. A child can play it well, and a grown man can never master it. Any single round of it is full of unexpected triumphs and seemingly perfect shots that end in disaster. It is almost a science, yet it is a puzzle with no answer.

Arnold Palmer

10. 'All Theory, Dear Friend, is Grey'

I found that Dunaverty had been well looked after by the older men who had stayed behind during World War II. Part of it had been requisitioned for agricultural purposes, but the course had been redesigned and, though now shorter, still consisted of eighteen interesting holes.

Throughout the six years of hostilities retired farmer James McNair had remained captain, and to him and his small committee a debt is owed by those of us who were abroad on other business. On our return we found that our membership had been maintained and that for another year we should be allowed to golf free of subscription. And the course, having been played on infrequently during the past six years – and having been spared the experimental excesses of too many greens conveners – was in wonderful condition. It was paradise regained, and we thanked our lucky stars that as far as golf was concerned Hitler had failed to interfere with a tradition of good husbandry. The little lights of civilized behaviour, never having been extinguished, flared up again in full brightness.

I discovered, almost with a lump in my throat, that what had occurred at Dunaverty had also been happening all over the country. The 'old boys' had kept faith with the younger generation. Using all the meagre means at their disposal they had preserved the courses. Even more important, they had nursed the golfing ethic through a crisis, so that it remained as strong and brotherly as it had ever been.

A story that came to us from the St Mellons Golf and Country Club near Cardiff, where play had often been interfered with by German bombers, provided an illustration of how the spirit of golf was maintained against all the odds.

Following queries and arguments among his intrepid members, Major G.L. Edsell, the secretary, drew up the following 'Rules', which were adopted by his committee and, indeed, in modified form, by the committees of several other clubs in the South of England.

1 Players are asked to collect bomb and shell splinters from the fairways to save these causing damage to the mowers.
2 In competitions, during gunfire or while bombs are falling, players may take cover without penalty for ceasing play.
3 The positions of known delayed action bombs are marked by red and white flags placed at reasonably, but not guaranteed, safe distances from the bombs.
4 Shell and/or bomb splinters on the greens may be removed without penalty. On the fairways or in bunkers within a club's length of a ball they may be moved without penalty, and no penalty shall be incurred if a ball is thereby caused to move accidentally.
5 A ball moved by enemy action may be replaced as near as possible to where it lay, or if lost or destroyed a ball may be dropped not nearer the hole without penalty.
6 A ball lying in any crater may be lifted and dropped not nearer the hole, preserving the line to the hole, without penalty.
7 A player whose stroke is affected by the simultaneous explosion of a bomb or shell, or by machine-gun fire, may play another ball from the same place. Penalty, one stroke.

Rule 7 is the one I like because it contains a hint of the steel which enabled the 'old boys' to show Hitler that whatever else he might destroy he was wasting his time as far as golf was concerned. Any golfer who betrayed a lack of moral fibre by flinching and duffing his shot because of bomb or shell or machine-gun fire had no claim to compassion. The one-stroke penalty was a proper reminder that to win a war hard discipline is required, even in the case of non-combatants.

I am sure Monty, my old general, would have approved. While he commanded us in North Africa, Sicily and Italy a story was current about an incident which occurred during his time with Southern Command in England. In his usual brash and uncompromising way he had initiated PT sessions for staff officers, each morning at six o'clock. As a rule these took the form of cross-country runs, in which Monty himself joined with hearty vigour. One cold and rainy dawn a certain colonel was missing from parade. Afterwards Monty sent for him.

'Not on PT this morning?'

'I was a bit under the weather, sir.'

'Why?'

'Well, you see, sir, we were having a party last night. A farewell party for an officer who is leaving us. A tradition in the mess, sir.'

'I see. You will be having another farewell party tonight. Yours. Good morning.'

Yes, Monty would have approved of the one-stroke penalty.

On coming back to Southend after the war, with a thankful heart, I found that in my absence Jock, aged 8, had begun to swing his way on to the golfing scene. From Duncan Watson, who acted as club steward and 'professional', Jean had got him some cut-down clubs, and now there was no problem about what he wanted to do outside of school. He wanted to play golf. And, luckily for his parents, when the weather was bad and golf was impossible he wanted to play the piano or, later, an accordion, his great exemplar being Primo Scala, whose accordion band flourished on 'Housewives' Choice'. I have already indicated my belief that good musicians are potentially good golfers. And the reverse may also be true. Jock's case would seem to offer evidence in support of the theory.

One of Jock's pals, in the same class at the local school, was Belle McCorkindale, who, even in those days, thirty-five years before she won the Ladies' British Open Amateur Championship, was of a tomboyish and athletic bent. She and Jock exchanged marbles, sorbo bouncers, pieces of old clocks, liquorice straps, home-made catapults and other oddments. When she was given a bicycle to ride to school she made a habit, at lunchtime, of cavorting round the playground with Jock on the handlebars.

Years later, when she discovered golf, she and Jock played together on Dunaverty, never imagining that one day her picture would be hung in a place of honour in the clubhouse, with the photocopy beneath it of an article Jock had written about her in the *Express*.

This article makes no reference to the fact that she and Jock, partnered in a mixed foursome competition, once achieved the highest score ever recorded for the 3rd hole at Dunaverty ('Scott's Holm'). Jock having sliced his drive on to the shore, they found their ball in the moat of a sandcastle. Twenty minutes and a sandpit later they holed out in 36. Being faithful golfers, even at a tender age, they had counted every stroke and given no thought to tearing up their card.

In the years following the war, with rationing and coal shortage only small irritants in the blessed peace, Jock struggled towards his Highers at school and I struggled to regain lost ground as a writer. Gradually we found our golf becoming more and more an absorbing interest, a therapy after studious hours indoors and a joy in itself. The heroic deeds of such as Fred Daly, Henry Cotton and Bobby Locke inspired us to work spasmodically at our own games, with articles in the golf magazines as added incentives. Then the name of John Panton began to appear in the lists of 'leading scores', and the fact that he was a Scot made us keener than ever to get our handicaps down.

At that time we had many other exemplars in the world of professional golf, some of them now remembered only by grey-haired veterans gossiping at the clubhouse bar. To fuel nostalgia and for the edification of younger golfers, I hereby present a list of the men described by Bobby Locke in 1953 as, in his view, 'the finest exponents with each particular club'.

Driver: Jimmy Thomson, then in his forties, a Scottish-born professional living in America, where he was regarded as 'the most consistent long driver in the world'.

2-Wood: Henry Cotton, at forty-five 'still one of Britain's leading players'.

3-Wood: Peter Thomson, a twenty-three-year-old Australian who, in Locke's opinion, was 'one of the most promising young golfers in the world'.

4-Wood: Herman Barron, an American, who, at forty-two, won the Tam o'Shanter tournament in 1946.

1-Iron: Sam Snead, then forty-one, one of the biggest money-winners in America, known as 'Slammin' Sam'.

2-Iron: Dr Cary Middlecoff, who only turned professional in 1947 at the age of twenty-nine and won the US Open two years later.

3-Iron: Jack Burke, Jnr, a young post-war 'discovery' in America, of whom Locke was sure a good deal would be heard in the future.

4-Iron: Byron Nelson, at forty, 'an outstanding iron player, even though he has now retired from big-time golf'.

5-Iron: Julius Boros, US Open Champion in 1952, still in his twenties.

6-Iron: Ed Oliver, better known as 'Porky' Oliver, who, at thirty-six, was a leading money-winner in the USA.

7-Iron: John Panton, thirty-seven, 'the Scottish professional who was outstanding as a boy golfer and is now one of the top British professionals'.

8-Iron: Ronnie White, a thirty-one-year-old solicitor and Britain's leading amateur, 'perhaps the best amateur golfer in the world'.

Wedge: Jimmy Demaret, forty-two, a leading American professional.

Sand-iron: Clayton Heafner, runner-up in the US Open, 1949 and 1951.

Putter: Ben Hogan. Said Locke: 'This forty-year-old player, back at the top after a serious motor crash, is one of the greatest American golfers of the century.'

Who are 'the finest exponents of each particular club' today?

As we worked at our golf Jock and I became particularly interested in a theory widely disseminated in journals of the period by Henry Cotton. This was that more length could be obtained by strengthening the hands and wrists and that the best way of achieving such strength was to swing iron clubs through thick rough and woods against a heavy rubber tyre: again and again and again to the very limit of endurance.

There is a sloping area on the left of the 3rd fairway at Dunaverty where the rough grows in tangled profusion, a green and smiling cemetery for shots which are hooked away in terror from the beach on the right. After the snow-bound winter and early spring of 1947 a mild April caused this area to resemble a miniature jungle: a place where David Bellamy might have found creatures never yet shown on television. Jock and I decided that this was probably the kind of rough Cotton had in mind and, in frenzied dedication, set about thinning it down with violent swings and grunting follow-throughs.

After only a few minutes of such exercise we were usually pouring with sweat and had to stop for a breather. But we persevered, finding hidden reserves of stamina. Then came an unlucky day when we were approached by the greens convener demanding what the hell we were doing and making it clear that if we continued with our vandalism he would report us to the committee. I was on the committee at the time; that year I was also the club champion. The situation, therefore, was one of considerable delicacy. Jock and I retired from the scene without a word but, I hope, with dignity.

Soon afterwards we found an old tractor tyre on the shore and used it to swing at with drivers on our own back green. Once again we strove, panting, to knock hell out of an almost immovable obstruction, and no doubt the muscular power in our hands and wrists was marginally augmented. But at the end of the day our golf seemed not to benefit at all. Indeed, Jock became affected by a soaring slice, a stroke which led eventually to the record high score by Belle and himself at the 3rd hole. I got into the habit, when my concentration faltered, of executing the lunging, hammer-throwing swing which betrays not only a disturbed mind but also a right side over-developed in relation to the left.

Years later Jock was completely cured of his slice when he had a course of six lessons from Hector Thomson, the veteran 'professor' at Machrihanish, who was also responsible for directing the course of Belle's early progress. But I still have rushes of blood to the head: crazy moments when my right arm and shoulder come scything down and the earth shakes and the ball leaps high and pitifully in the direction of mid-on. As a rule it vanishes into bracken or whins. Occasionally, however, it lands in the quivering quagmire near the standing stone at the 9th, into which not only many balls have disappeared but also several clubs. As a boy I assisted in the rescue of a child from its gurgling depths. He had refused to let us play with his football, so we had thrown him in. But that is another story, irrelevant to golf.

It is now apparent to me that in attempting to follow Cotton's advice Jock and I were like sick men swallowing medicine without the benefit of qualified medical supervision. Jock did the sensible thing at last and sought help from a professional. I preferred to work out my own salvation. This was a mistake and possibly the reason why I never became a first-class golfer.

MEMO

All theory, dear friend, is grey, but the golden tone of actual life springs ever green.

Johann Wolfgang von Goethe

11. Mighty Men Which Were of Old

Finding that despite all our efforts to practise the theories of the experts, our games showed little, if any, improvement, I suggested to Jock that it might be good for our morale if we went to one of the big tournaments and actually saw our heroes in action. Was it not possible that some of their skill might rub off on to us? Jean agreed it was a good idea, and so, for our summer holiday in 1950, we journeyed to Troon for the Open Championship.

Those were the days before tented villages, catering marquees, hospitality tents, luxurious port-a-loos and electronic scoreboards. Beer and sandwich tents might be located in obscure corners, with, in the same areas, some flapping hessian which inadequately screened furtive queues of bladder-emptying males. (What of the ladies? Bordering many fairways were thick woods and clumps of whins.)

As tournaments progressed no arrangements were made for the leading contenders to go out last, their playing positions depending upon a daily draw. This made it difficult to find your hero on the course and even more difficult to discover how he was playing, because few scoreboards were in evidence.

The courses were not roped off. Spectators were allowed to follow on the players' heels, to scramble all over the fairways and to sit around the greens.

It was not until 1962 tha the first tented village, perhaps without all the refinements common to the modern scene, was erected at a golf tournament. This was at the Senior Service tournament at Dalmahoy, near Edinburgh, where, with goggling eyes, we were confronted by what seemed like acres of shining white canvas, under which were housed restaurants, bars, closed-circuit television, hot and cold running water and flush toilets. We were also offered tubular steel 'stands' in which you could actually sit, and information boards strategically placed around the course. A new era for spectators had begun.

At this tournament I also saw for the first time a young and fresh-faced Raymond Floyd, then serving his apprenticeship on the American circuit but currently trying his luck in a few European events in order to gain experience. On the same occasion, at Dalmahoy, a dark-haired, chubby, keen-eyed youth was pointed out to me. 'A future champion,' my mentor prophesied. The youth's name was Bernard Gallacher.

But at Troon in 1950 all this was in the future. Jean and Jock and I galloped round the course, hugely enjoying an intimate view of all the great men in action. If, at the time, we were uncertain about the scores, we had a chance to confirm them each evening on a 'leader-board' situated near the clubhouse. Though catering tents within the playing area were few we carried sandwiches and flasks in the bags containing our rainwear and never went hungry or thirsty. Our main objective was to study the techniques of the masters, and this we were able to do, at satisfyingly close quarters. The lack of other facilities did not worry us: we knew no better.

In the field were the men whose names, for us, had become magic. Cotton had been Open Champion three times: in 1934 at Sandwich, in 1937 at Carnoustie and in 1948 at Muirfield. With grim jaw and steely eyes he had stood up to the Americans in matchplay as no other contemporary British player had done. His reputation was so high that clubs bearing his name sold in thousands. And as he was the first professional golfer to wear a left-hand glove, I have no doubt that those with his name on them sold in millions.

Locke was a young South African. Once a slender stripling but now, after war service with the air force, more stoutly built and of a dignified mien, he had emerged from golfing obscurity to take second place to Sam Snead in the 1946 Open at St Andrews. Thereafter, with a swing and style which challenged every tenet of orthodoxy, he had steadily climbed – in Britain and America – to a peak of achievement in 1949, when, at Sandwich, he had become Open Champion.

We recognized that luck had been with him on that occasion, because his victory came only after a play-off with Harry Bradshaw, and had the stout and jovial Irishman not found his ball inside a broken bottle and taken 6 on a hole where otherwise he would almost certainly have carded a 4, he and not Locke would have been the champion. But in some indefinable way Locke was a charismatic personality, whose white visor, Royal and Ancient tie tucked into the buttons of a white business shirt and voluminous poacher's plus-fours appealed to the imagination.

Fred Daly was a personality, too, whistling down the fairways like a bucolic cherub, and it is difficult to understand why he never became a 'big name' with the press like some of his contemporaries. Was it because he came from Northern Ireland and had no high-powered publicity men behind him? Was it because he showed no burning desire to compete abroad?

His record was an outstanding one. As we watched him play at Troon, his obvious enjoyment of the game contrasted with the grim determination displayed by such as Frank Stranahan and other Americans in the field. We remembered how in 1947 he had become not only the Open Champion, at Hoylake, but also Matchplay Champion at Royal Lytham, the first winner of both titles in the same season since Braid in 1911, the year Daly was born.

His victory in the Matchplay championship had been gained at the expense of none other than the great Henry Cotton, and the manner of it still made us chuckle with admiration. Jack Magowan of the *Belfast Telegraph* has published a description of the turning point of the game in Daly's own words.

I had been two up on Henry leaving the 14th green. The 15th at Lytham in those days was a par-5 hole spanning most of 460 yards. We both hit good drives, Henry just a fraction longer than me. With the wind blowing across the hole, the second shot was always a wood, but I decided to try a bluff. 'Give me that battered old cleek,' I told my caddie, loudly enough for all to hear, especially Henry, then proceeded to slam a big shot full bore under the wind and straight at the flag.

It was one of the best shots I ever played in tournament golf. At the same time, I wasn't sure whether the ball was home or not, and neither was Henry. This much I was sure of, however: the maestro wouldn't stoop to hitting a wooden club after I had hit an iron. And if I couldn't make it home with an iron, then he couldn't.

The ploy worked. Cotton played a 2-iron, hooked his ball disastrously off-line and, in the end, conceded the hole to Daly's perfect birdie.

Daly was now dormy three. For Cotton it was curtains.

Jack Magowan then goes on to say that 'the clubs Daly used in that history-making era are among his most treasured possessions. They include that famous cleek or '2-X iron' as Fred calls it, a shallow-faced club which only one player in a thousand can ever use. With it, the wiry, steel-wristed Portrush man could have knocked the cap off your head at 200 yards' range. Sam Snead wasn't exaggerating when he once called Fred 'a prince among long-iron players'.

Daly always enjoyed his golf. He still does, and in the proper spirit. A few years ago some St Andrews University students went to Belfast to play a team of local members at Balmoral. One of their opponents was introduced to them as 'Willie Frew, our bar steward'. To the young Scots' astonishment 'Willie' took an iron off the first tee, struck the ball yards past anybody else and then calmly went on to do the first six holes in three under fours.

Eventually the truth dawned on one at least of the St Andrews men that an Irish joke had been played on them. 'If this guy is a steward here,' he said, 'I'm sure Fred Daly isn't playing today!'

Our other hero at Troon was John Panton, the sturdy Scot whose ambition had once been to become a professional footballer but who, after war service abroad, had settled down at Glenbervie as a professional golfer. In 1948, at Prestwick, he had won his first Scottish Championship, in 1949 his second at Nairn; and it had become apparent to us that here was an exciting new star, a worthy successor to his famous countrymen, Braid and Herd. And, indeed, as it turned out, John was to become Scottish Champion six more times, his eighth and last victory being shared with Eric Brown at Cruden Bay in 1966.

It may be interesting to note here that the 'Master Models' which provided fame and fortune for the once obscure club-making firm of John Letters at Hillington near Glasgow were first publicized with the names of Fred Daly, Dai Rees and John Panton. They sold worldwide, offering powerful opposition to the Cotton models manufactured by Nicholls of Leven. At one time I played with a Letters Daly driver. When, gaining years and losing strength, I was persuaded to exchange it for a carbon-shafted 'Wilson Staff' I felt as a man must feel who has jilted a faithful sweetheart for a smart young sophisticate of uncertain temper. Where had all the comfort gone?

That year at Troon two of the men we had come to watch, Cotton and Panton, were soon out of contention. Indeed, Daly began none too well, either, scoring a 75 and 72 on the first two days; and Locke had disappointed us a little by handing in a somewhat flawed 72 following a brilliant opening round of 69.

Locke himself remembers what happened on that second day. 'After being one under fours at the end of four holes, I took a 6 at the short 5th hole before 8000 people. This was a great shock, and as I lifted my ball out of the hole, I decided I must be satisfied at having won the Open once. But I was determined not to give up, scored four birdies in the next six holes and finished that round in 72. No one knows how near I was to giving up after that 6.'

The short 5th at Troon is called 'Greenan', after a castle, now in ruins, built by the Earls of Cassilis near Ayr. It is 194 yards long. Among the marram grass immediately front right and left of the green are menacing bunkers, and it was into one of these that Locke's tee-shot disappeared. Jean and Jock and I were among the 8000 who watched with dismay as he struggled to get out of it. But his expression before and after this traumatic experience never altered. His calm, unhurried movements completely camouflaged what he was thinking.

In his rise to the top as a professional golfer Locke had acquired a stoical philosophy, best described in his own words:

In my younger days I always got excited. I got excited during the 1946 Open at St Andrews when I saw that I had a chance of winning. I started to walk fast and that geared me up. My concentration began to suffer. I made poor shots and lost in the end to Sam Snead. When I congratulated Sam his reply is something I have never forgotten. He said, quietly, 'Thanks, Bob, but it is just another tournament.' So that was how Sam Snead regarded the British Open – or any other big competition – 'Just another tournament'. Obviously this was his tournament temperament, and I decided that the sooner I acquired the same outlook the better. Ever since then I have moved and played at a steady pace, maintaining my rhythm, keeping my emotions to myself. I have been called many things – 'poker face', 'muffin face', etc. – but that is due to a determination never to convey my inner feelings to an opponent.

On the final day at Troon, Locke put all thoughts of the dreaded 5th behind him and put together two majestic rounds of 70 and 68. I remember him, on his last round, marching along the 16th fairway towards the green, round which we stood – and sat – breathlessly admiring the shot he had just played to within feet of the flag. When he holed the putt we broke into loud applause. He touched his white visor in grave acknowledgement, and then, without even the hint of a smile, paced coolly towards the 17th tee. Jock and I agreed that had it been us we should have been dancing with joy. Jean said: 'But neither of you will ever win the Open.' Feminine logic is always devastating.

In the outcome, however, it was a close-run thing. Locke won the championship with a total of 279. Second was the stout and smiling Roberto de Vicenzo from Argentina with 281, and sharing third place, to our delight, was Fred Daly, who came into brave contention with final rounds of 69 and 66. The only other 'last-day surge' I have seen to compare with it was when Jack Nicklaus scored 66 and 68 at St

Andrews in 1964 in a vain but glorious attempt to catch Tony Lema.

So two of our heroes at least had not let us down. And, as a bonus, we had added two more heroes to our list, de Vicenzo and Rees, the little Welshman who had led after the first two days and finished equal third with Daly. From then on the golfing exploits of Dai Rees became as exciting for Jock as the accordion playing of Primo Scala.

I remember well two minor events which occurred in that 1950 Open at Troon.

The first concerns de Vicenzo, who, in the final round, at the 123-yard hole, the 'Postage Stamp', found his tee-shot plugged in a bunker, declared it unplayable and, accepting a penalty of loss of distance only, as the rule then allowed, went back to the tee, hit his second on the green and holed the putt for a 3. Some time later this experimental rule was scrapped by the Royal and Ancient, and Jim Greenlees, that staunch supporter of the principle of 'play the ball where it lies', expressed himself at the Annual General Meeting of the Dunaverty Golf Club as being 'mightily relieved'.

My second memory is of the terrible disaster which befell Hermann Tissies, a German amateur, at the same 8th hole. We did not witness it, and in a way I am glad of this, because intrusion into private grief can be a soul-scarifying experience. At the same time, we listened with ghoulish relish to the tale told by a friend who had seen it all.

Hermann put his tee-shot into a bunker on the left of the green. Four times he swung his sand-wedge and failed to get the ball out. His fifth attempt hurled sand high into the air; the ball soared up, too, but unhappily ran into a bunker on the right of the green. With German tenacity Hermann again swung his sand-wedge. Once, twice, three, four times he did so and still had not escaped from the deep and evil trap. But again, on his fifth shot, the ball flew up, only to land in the original bunker on the other side of the green. By now, I imagine, silent screams were echoing in Hermann's head. Being a faithful golfer, however, he gritted his teeth and continued to perform his task. This time he got the ball out on his third stroke and, by some miracle, holed the putt. Score for the hole, 15. He did not qualify.

While labouring in the bowels of the big bunker on the left of the 8th fairway at Dunaverty, I always think of Hermann and am comforted.

When we returned home from Troon we found that our 'investment' in the Open brought immediate 'dividends'. Our scores improved. I had a round in the high sixties; Jock achieved his first 'level fours'. What had happened, we decided – after discussion and careful analysis – was that we had acquired, through observation, the rhythmic swings and impeccable timing of the professionals. The secret of golf was ours. We should never look back.

Unhappily, after a week or two, we seemed to lose the secret. Our old faults and failings returned, and golf again became a 'varmint game'.

But we made up our minds about one thing. Every Open that was played in Scotland we should attend, in an effort, as it were, to recharge our batteries. And through the years, Jean and I as spectators and Jock eventually as a reporter, we have done just that, with a Ryder Cup and other important tournaments on the side.

Each time, after those excursions, my golf has been better, probably because the style of the professionals reminded me of Joyce Wethered's wise words about being aware of the weight of the clubhead throughout the swing. And each time the improvement has lasted longer. Perhaps, by the time I am 90 – and the occasional impulse to do the ball a savage injury no longer recurs – the old faults will not come back at all.

MEMO

Speak of the moderns without contempt, and of the ancients without idolatry.

Earl of Chesterfield

12. 'Let Us Now Praise Famous Men'

In respect of all the Opens played in Scotland after 1950 'the table of my memory' is lavishly furnished. There was Ben Hogan's victory in 1953 at Carnoustie, which he achieved with all the odds against him.

When first it was announced that the four times US Open winner was crossing the Atlantic in order to add our Open to his awesome record, many golfers in Britain hoped that this apparently arrogant Texan might get his 'comeuppance'. At the time we had heard little of the motor-car accident which, in 1949, had racked his body almost to extinction and of his dour battle back to physical fitness. We had not known much either about his lovely wife, Valerie, whose life he had saved in the accident, and whose influence on his career had been so strong and steadfast. Nor did we realize that the cold and somewhat blustery weather which prevailed at Carnoustie would exacerbate the stiffness and pain in his muscles. And only after the championship was over were we told that on the second day he had contracted 'flu. We did notice that during the final two rounds he played with two sweaters on top of his favourite turtle-necked pullover, but we thought this was only because of the uncomfortable weather.

Before this, however, we had begun to change our minds about the quiet, grim-faced little man. After watching one of his practice rounds, which had rendered us almost dumb with admiration for the quality of his shot-making, Valerie was pointed out to us among the crowd behind the 18th green. It occurred to me then that if he could retain the love and devotion of such a beautiful woman there must be more to Hogan than appeared on the surface. And as the tournament progressed stories about his accident began to come through, and another was told which revealed that underneath that grey exterior there lurked a sense of humour. To a fellow professional he had remarked: 'I understand the tees we are using here are called "tiger" tees. I believe it. They are so far back among the heather and gorse that every time I drive I expect a tiger to jump out at me.'

By the time he teed off to play his final round, Jean and Jock and I, far from wishing him ill, found ourselves among the growing multitude of his supporters. We had recognized in him not only a man with strength of character above the ordinary but also the most dedicated of golfers.

An additional interest for us was that on the last day he was partnered by Hector Thomson, winner of the Amateur Championship at St Andrews in 1936 and also of the Scottish Professional Championship at Gullane in 1953. One of the famous golfing family of Thomsons of Machrihanish, our near neighbours in Kintyre, Hector was known to us personally.

Rushing for vantage points, we watched Hogan complete with clinical accuracy a closing round of 68. This was a record for the course, and it gave him the championship by four strokes from the four who tied for second place: Frank Stranahan, Dai Rees, Peter Thomson and Antonio Cerda from Argentina.

Two interviews appeared in a magazine after the Carnoustie Open. One was with Hector Thomson, who had been asked about Hogan's apparent coldness. 'Why, for example,' asked the reporter, 'did he seem so indifferent when the spectators were cheering him on?'

'He was anything but indifferent,' was Hector's reply. 'Every time they applauded one of his shots he'd murmur "thank you". You had to be close to hear it, but it was always there.' Then, he added: 'He's a fine sportsman as well as a great golfer.'

Hector should know. He also is a fine sportsman and a great golfer.

The other interview was with Hogan himself. He was neither a hypocrite nor in any way sanctimonious, yet he concluded it by saying: 'I don't think anybody does anything unless the Lord is with them. I think the Lord has let me win so many tournaments for a purpose. I hope that purpose is to give courage to all those people who are sick or injured and broken in body as I once was.'

It was at Carnoustie that a bright new golfing star – and, glory be, a Scot at that – made himself known to us. His name was Eric Brown, and his talent, we discovered, was as sharp as a sword-blade. In the first two rounds of the 1953 Open he scored 71 each time and, indeed, going into the final day shared the lead with Dai Rees. Youth and inexperience may have caused him to fall away slightly on the last day with successive rounds of 75, but to finish equal ninth with Peter Alliss was a splendid start to a splendid career. The great John Panton had now a home-bred rival worthy of his steel. In the next fifteen years Eric Brown was to win the Scottish Professional Championship eight times, including the tie with Panton at Cruden Bay in 1966.

To our delight Eric proved to be a tigerish opponent for the Americans. He played in four successive Ryder Cup matches, and his record in the singles is remarkable. In 1953 at Wentworth he beat Lloyd Mangrum 2 up. In 1955 at Palm Springs he beat Jerry Barber 3 and 2. In 1957 at Lindrick, near Sheffield, he beat Tommy Bolt 4 and 3. And in 1959 at Palm Desert, California, he beat Cary Middlecoff 4 and 3.

When he was elected as non-playing captain of the Great Britain and Ireland Ryder Cup team at Royal Birkdale in 1969 his keenly competitive and even aggressive approach resulted in a drawn match against opposition which included Jack Nicklaus, Lee Trevino, Billy Casper, Ray Floyd and Gene Littler, all at the height of their powers. Jean and I watched the match on television, our nerves stabilized only marginally by frequent cups of tea. Mine, I confess, were sometimes reinforced by a 'cinder', especially on that last afternoon when the whole outcome depended upon the result of the Jacklin versus Nicklaus game. But Jock was there, reporting, and he will tell the full story in a later chapter.

That year, 1969, saw the first appearance in the Ryder Cup of Bernard Gallacher. At Dalmahoy in 1962 a prophecy had been made to me that he would become a champion. The prophecy had now come true. At Royal Birkdale he dealt dourly and efficiently with Lee Trevino, beating him 4 and 3, and I realized that here was another Scot plentifully endowed with the spirit of *nemo me impune lacessit*. Strangely enough, both he and Eric are natives of the same town in West Lothian, near Edinburgh. Can there be something special about the air of Bathgate?

While watching Eric Brown striding over a golf course, arms swinging straight, aquiline nose pointing like a retriever's in a lean, almost cadaverous face, body bent slightly forward as if he grudged even the few minutes of inaction between shots, I always used to wish he could have been a member of Dunaverty Players, my Amateur Drama Club. Any villainous parts originally played by Basil Rathbone would have been his for the asking; and as a pirate in a pantomime he would have been a hero to anybody with a youthful heart between the ages of nine and ninety.

An incident which took place in the Ryder Cup match at Lindrick in 1957 may provide a clue to his competitive calibre. In the singles he was selected to play the top match against the legendary Tommy Bolt, from Oklahoma: 'legendary' because of the many stories concerning his volatile temper which are exchanged in clubhouses throughout the world. According to one American golf writer Tommy was Vesuvius: 'You never knew whether it was going to be a nice sunny day or the last days of Pompeii.'

Throwing clubs was his way not only of expressing disgust at his own mistakes but also of releasing tension. One year, in the US Open, at Cherry Hills in Denver, he threw his driver so far into a pond that one observer claimed that if it had been a discus Tommy would have won a gold medal at the Olympic Games. During another tournament he had to pay a deep-sea diver to swim down a canal and rescue his driver from twenty fathoms.

While playing in the Australian Seniors Championship at the Manly Club in Sydney, his raucous voice was heard calling upon the Lord to damn and burn in hell a particular bunker that had spoilt his round.

'And don't send your Son down!' he yelled upwards to the sky. 'This is a man's job!'

In the end, after a season punctuated by numerous fines for misbehaviour on the course, the US PGA appointed him chairman of the Tour's 'good conduct' committee. This, it appeared, was like giving a poacher the gamekeeper's job. In spite of all the evidence to the contrary, however, Tommy Bolt was a faithful golfer. One of his first acts in his new post was to fine himself a hundred dollars for club-throwing.

He was an intimidating character. So was Eric Brown. I saw part of their aforementioned match at Lindrick in 1957 on television. As I watched, no words were exchanged, but the way they eyed each other reminded me of an encounter I had once observed between two stags in a Highland glen. As the match neared its end the inevitable happened. Two holes down, Bolt hit an approach shot fat. Infuriated with himself, he uttered a sound which mixed a roar with a scream and hurled his club into an adjoining wood. Brown permitted himself a snarling smile, shaped up carefully to his ball and struck it on to the green. Then he, too, roared and screamed and hurled *his* club into the wood. Soon afterwards, all passion spent, they shook hands on the 15th green.

About this time I was asked by the *Glasgow Evening Citizen* to script a cartoon series in which Eric featured as the wise professional giving instruction to a young golfer aiming for the Amateur Championship. I found Eric both straightforward and friendly. But I took care never to argue too strongly with him, especially when he turned that steely glance in my direction.

There was one picture in which I had suggested that the position of the young amateur's grip would lead to a slice.

Eric took one look at it. 'Slice be damned!' he said, or rather, spat. 'That grip would make him hook to hell!'

I said: 'I don't know about that – '

'Hooked to hell!' he said, leaning forward with menace.

'Okay,' I said, quietly. 'Hooked to hell!'

But I am still not sure that Eric was right. When I held the club in the manner shown, I sliced. Of course, as this book is intended to demonstrate, in golf one man's mean can be another's poison.

In 1955 the Open was held at St Andrews. Jean and Jock

and I stayed for the week at Elie's Golf Hotel, thirteen miles
away. We left the Mull of Kintyre with rain lashing across the
bonnet of the car. On the Monday morning the weather
cleared, the sun came out and a heat-wave settled over Fife.

Shirt-sleeved, Jock and I played golf on the Elie course,
which after the extraordinary first hole where you drive over a
drab green hill into the unknown (when the starter tells you),
opens out into a beautiful seaside links.

We saw some of the qualifying rounds in the Open and
were present at the 18th green of the New Course at St
Andrews when Frank Jowle came in with a 63, a record score
which was to inspire a sub-editor on *The Times* to perpetrate
the headline, CHEEK BY JOWLE.

When the Open proper began we commuted daily to the
Old Course and, daily, the sun shone down from a friendly
sky. We panted and sweated as we followed our heroes,
marvelling at their accuracy and power.

On the final day, having expended most of our energy, we
decided to take up early stances on the road above and to the
right of the 18th green. There we stood – hour after hour in
fact, though we remained unconscious of time – while all the
competitors finished their rounds and news came filtering in
from the course about the fortunes of such as Johnny Fallon,
Frank Jowle, Bobby Locke, Ken Bousefield and the holder
himself, Peter Thomson.

We ate our rolls and drank our coffee from a flask.
Complete strangers came rushing up to tell us that Fallon was
burning up the course, that Locke had missed a short putt at
one of the holes around the turn, that Thomson had taken a 7
at one of the holes coming in. In turn we passed on the news to
our neighbours.

We trained our binoculars on the big scoreboard among the
tents on the right of the first fairway; and as the leading scores
kept changing we ignored the tiredness in our legs and sighed
with content. It was going to be a close race, and we were
there, looking down at the 18th green, in the best possible
place to observe a dramatic finish.

And, even after five days of it, the sun still beat down with
such strength that at one stage a young friend of Jock's eased

himself out of the crowd and pressed his bare arms against the glass of a shop window behind us. 'To cool me down,' he explained from a red and peeling face.

At last we saw Thomson driving off from the distant 18th tee. The word was that he had recovered magnificently from that ugly 7 and required only a 5 to win from Fallon. He took a 4 with stylish ease, and, as the applause died away a grey mist came creeping in over the sea. Soon the sun disappeared and the deserted course was covered as if by a temporary dust-sheet.

It grew cold. We trudged round towards the beach to find the car. Another Open was behind us, our legs were stiff and we had a feeling of anticlimax. But as we picked our way back to Elie through a maze of traffic, with a pleasant drink and a substantial meal in the offing, contentment returned. Next week, on Dunaverty, we should put into practice all we had learned, especially from Peter Thomson, whose swing was so simple and easy that it seemed anyone could emulate it.

As we knew in our hearts, however, and as it eventually transpired, anyone could not. Simplicity and easiness in any artistic endeavour is gained only at the expense of long and arduous practice. Added to which there must always be that elusive touch of genius.

In 1957 the Open again took place at St Andrews. This time Jean and I went alone, because Jock had begun his two years of soldiering with the Argylls on national service. On the last day we again stood on the road overlooking the 18th green and saw Bobby Locke win by three strokes from Peter Thomson, with Eric Brown in third place.

I noticed that on the last green Locke marked his ball, which had come to rest as if guided by a magnet about four feet from the hole. It being directly on his partner's line, he placed a marker not immediately behind it but the length of his putter-head to the side. What I did *not* notice was that when his turn came to putt he replaced the ball not in its original position but beside the marker, an inch or two away. Bravely he sank the putt, and the cheers rang out, and he touched his white cap in sober acknowledgement.

He showed no sign of emotion then, but what must his

feelings have been when it was pointed out to him that he had sunk his last putt from the wrong place? Technically there was a case for his disqualification. There was no question, however, of his ball having been replaced *nearer* the hole, and the spirit of equity, which is the soul of golf, in the end prevailed. He was allowed to keep the championship, as he deserved to, and not one of his fellow professionals for whom large sums of money were at stake said another word about it.

The whole incident shows, I believe, that while maintaining outward calm Locke could become as dazed with excitement at the prospect of winning another Open as I am at the prospect of winning another monthly medal. Old 'muffin face' was human after all. We liked him the better for it.

In 1959 at Muirfield, we saw another champion whose reactions were much more recognizably human. I can never forget the expression of utter misery on Gary Player's face as he walked off after his final round having just taken an unhappy 6 at the last hole. He had scored an otherwise brilliant 68 in his pursuit of Flory van Donck of Belgium and Scotland's Fred Bullock; but it seemed to him that he needed a 66 to win and that by carding a double bogey at the 18th he had – in his own words – 'blown his chances'. Not only that: he had betrayed weakness in a crisis, an idea abhorrent to his ambitious nature. I was told that for the next hour, as he waited in the clubhouse for van Donck and Bullock to come in, he sat silent and sad, eyes brimming with tears.

Then, for Player, a miracle appeared to happen. Both van Donck and Bullock faltered with scores of 73 and 74 respectively, which gave them both aggregates of 286. But Player's aggregate was 284. To his incredulous delight he realized that he had won the Open.

He rushed from the clubhouse out on to the first fairway, where the presentation ceremony was due to be held. Officials had not yet appeared. The table was empty of trophies. The long bench on which successful competitors would sit was also empty. Only a few spectators had begun to gather. But Player seemed oblivious of his isolation. There he sat, alone on a long bench, staring fixedly ahead. He looked young, frail, vulnerable and almost pathetic. And yet, behind it all, I sensed the steel-hard determination that in the next decade was to make him the most formidable matchplayer in the world.

Did his momentary loss of concentration at the 18th hole at Muirfield teach him a lesson he was never afterwards to forget?

Twelve months later, in 1960, when St Andrews hosted the Centenary Open, Arnold Palmer appeared in glory before our very eyes: an extrovert, smiling, trouser-hitching character (would he have been more comfortable wearing gallowses?) who was immediately recognizable as a human being. His 'army' in America was no more fervent than that which he gathered around him in Britain. The ferocity of his 'charges' had been well publicized before his arrival, and we were to witness a dramatic example at St Andrews when, in the final round, he hunted Kel Nagle of Australia as a greyhound hunts a hare.

That final round was due to be played on the afternoon of the third day. At the end of the morning round, however, a furious rainstorm burst over the course. I remember standing with Jean under the awning of a tent on the right of the first fairway, with rain smacking down on the canvas above and pouring off it like a small Niagara. The fairways of the 1st and 18th became shallow lakes upon which raindrops splashed and leaped with such vigour that they caused a kind of crystal mist. Through the mist we saw a deep pool forming in the Valley of Sin immediately in front of the 18th green, a pool fed by water seeping in from the roadway above and cascading down the steps of the Royal and Ancient clubhouse. It looked as if officials might have to consider the building of an ark.

But the storm soon passed. Fire engines came to pump out water from the Valley of Sin, and platoons of men with mops, squeegees and buckets were deployed on the course. We waited, shaking out our umbrellas and hoping against hope that play might be resumed. At last, however, came the inevitable announcement. The afternoon round had been cancelled. The showdown between Nagle and Palmer would be postponed until the following day.

And what a showdown it proved to be.

In the manner of most seaside links based on thirsty sand, the Old Course had quickly recovered from its soaking and now smiled innocently under the sun. At the beginning Nagle led by four shots with an aggregate of 207. Like the good professional he was, he played on with steadiness and cheerful courage to record a 71 and a total of 278, until then the best ever Open score at St Andrews. But thanks to some brilliant play, including a 3 at the treacherous Road Hole (the 17th), Palmer found himself standing on the 18th tee requiring a 3 to tie for the championship. That he failed to get it, by a matter of inches only, takes nothing away from the quality of his 68. And it reflects credit upon Nagle, who gritted his teeth and, in the end, defied the awesome 'charge'.

Our next Open was also at St Andrews, in 1964, when Palmer was joined by a 'young pretender' to his eminence in the person of Jack Nicklaus. With eyes of chilly blue, a crew-cut and stocky build, he did not appear at first to possess the charisma so evident in Palmer. A few in 'Arnie's Army' treated him with open hostility. Not until five years later, during the Ryder Cup match at Royal Birkdale, was Nicklaus's true character appreciated. Then, at a stroke – or non-stroke, as it happened – even his severest critics 'could scarce forbear to cheer' and he became one of the most popular and respected golfers in history. (But that is another story, which, in due course, will be told by Jock.)

If, in 1964 at St Andrews, Nicklaus did not have an immediate appeal as a personality, his worth as a golfer was amply demonstrated. For me, however, his performance was overshadowed by that of a stranger, who, with his disciplined temperament, his slow and elegant swing and graceful poise as he followed through, remains my favourite champion. He came to our notice like a comet riding through a dull sky. Sadly, he left us in a trail of glory, never to return. He was Tony Lema.

In my own case, that Open began on a high and happy note. To Ian McColl and Drew Rennie, editor and features editor respectively of the *Scottish Daily Express*, then at a high peak of popularity, I had sold the idea of a murder mystery serial, set in St Andrews and reading like a continuous news story: a story which would be linked in time with the Open by including comments concerning its progress in each instalment. (It was later published in book form with the title *Murder at the Open*.)

The first instalment was published on the Monday, when practice rounds were being played. Jean and I were following a four-ball which included Palmer and Phil Rodgers, who, the year before at Royal Lytham and St Annes, had been beaten in a play-off for the championship by Bob Charles of New Zealand. At the 17th, as he played out of the Road Bunker, I heard Rodgers call out to Palmer: 'Say, Arnie, according to the papers they found a body in here this morning!' I was thrilled, as only an author can be, by such evidence that what I had written was actually being read.

But soon my interest in the fictional drama of *Murder at the Open* was suceeded by an even greater interest in the living drama of the championship itself. What I wrote about it at the time has the merit of immediacy, in respect of both fact and emotion, and so I quote from it here, in full.

In July 1964, at St Andrews, Tony Lema saw the Old Course for the first time. At the beginning he must have felt afraid, for that week the old Lady of Fife was windswept and cantankerous, in a fiercely difficult mood. Powermen like Jack Nicklaus and Roberto de Vicenzo fought ruggedly to impress her; and impress her they did, de Vicenzo with a score of 76 at the height of the gale and Nicklaus with a record-equalling 66 in the third round. But Lema treated her in a different way – quietly, respectfully, with steadfast gallantry. And in the end, the Old Lady being entirely feminine, it was the handsome, stylish Lema who stole her heart.

He stood outside the Royal and Ancient Clubhouse holding the Trophy. 'Last night,' I heard him say, 'I went down on my knees and prayed. And God has been good to me, because now, for the first time, I can call myself a champion.'

He had come a long way from his orphan boyhood in California, from jobs in the shipyards, in the steel works and the canneries, from spare time work as a caddie to help the family income.

At 20 he decided to try his luck as a golf professional and 'follow the sun'. Life became an exciting adventure – too exciting, perhaps, for a young man travelling from town to town on the tournament circuit; a young man, moreover, with the warm blood of Portugal in his veins, friendly, kind and sociable by nature.

At first he won few prizes. In his own words, his golf was lousy. But he imagined that social pleasures might compensate in some way for his bad golf.

Then suddenly, as he said to himself, he came round to thinking that there must be more to golf – more to life in fact – than 'chasing broads and liquour . With cool courage he imposed on himself a hard course of self-discipline. To a man of his temperament this couldn't have been easy, and nobody was surprised when occasionally he still panicked in a crisis and was still inclined to live it up as an antidote to failure on the golf course.

But he stuck it out. In 1962 he found himself leading the field after the third round of the Orange County Open in America. Pressmen offered him glasses of beer, but he waved them away. 'If I win tomorrow,' he said, 'we'll drink champagne.'

He did win, after a play-off with Bob Rosburg. He also kept his word about the champagne, and the grateful pressmen christened him Champagne Tony.

In 1963 he married, and marriage brought confidence: not the confidence that comes out of a champagne bottle but the confidence of self-knowledge and self-restraint. He began to take the big prizes, including one of 23,000 dollars at the Cleveland Open early in 1964. But though he didn't know it, the ultimate test of his inward discipline was still to come.

After two rounds of the Open at St Andrews, he was in front by nine strokes from Nicklaus. It looked like a walk-over. But on the morning of the final day the Old Lady of Fife withdrew her smile. He reached the 6th hole two over 4s and saw that across at the 12th – on the same huge double green – Nicklaus's scoreboard was showing minus 5 in red chalk, five *under* 4s. Seven of Lema's nine strokes had already gone. I watched from a high bank, suffering with him. His glimpse of that board must have twisted a knife in his guts.

But what was his reaction? Panic? A smile and a shrug to camouflage despair? None of these. Calmly and faultlessly Champagne Tony played the next five holes in level 3s, bringing his score back to three under 4s and re-establishing an unassailable lead.

Here was a man who admitted having been born 'on the wrong side of the tracks', but who now showed that his natural style had been buttressed and dignified by patiently acquired self-control. The Old Lady, having tested him, smiled again. She knew a champion when she saw one.

About two years later, in America, Lema's private plane crashed, killing himself and his wife. His death drained from golf a little of its grace.

In the next few years Jean and I saw Jack Nicklaus win the Open at Muirfield in 1966, when that lovely course for both golfers and spectators had a rush of hay to its head. We saw Player win again at Carnoustie in 1968. To our lasting regret, however, we were absent from Royal Lytham when Jacklin became champion in 1969; but we followed his progress on television and, along with many others, wept tears of joy as he sank his last putt and shook hands with Bob Charles.

We were at St Andrews in 1970 when Nicklaus, discarding his jerkin on the 18th tee, hit a mighty drive through the green to beat the unfortunate Sanders in a play-off. At Muirfield in 1972 we watched Lee Trevino flick a careless sand-iron shot on to the 17th green and, by inadvertently holing it, destroy Jacklin's chance of winning a second championship. 'God,' he reminded us at the 18th, 'is a Mexican!'

At Troon in 1973 we were broiled by the sun and soaked by the rain as Tom Weiskopf became champion by three strokes from Neil Coles and Johnny Miller. Then, neatly and smilingly, Tom Watson appeared at Carnoustie in 1975. Not only did he beat Jack Newton of Australia in a play-off; he also laid down a challenge to Nicklaus's supremacy as Nicklaus himself had done to Palmer's years before. At Turnberry in 1977 Watson won what sub-editors called 'the great duel in the sun'. But in 1978 at St Andrews, Nicklaus sharply reasserted his authority. At Troon, in 1982, Watson won his third Open on Scottish soil and became an 'honorary Scotsman'.

One thing we learned on our travels: all the great professionals (as in art, literature, music, the theatre and sport in general) are amateurs at heart.

Ever since Lema's victory in 1964 Jean and I have attended the Opens as carefree spectators and left all the reporting to Jock. In the following five chapters he recalls some of his personal experiences.

MEMO

Watson and Nicklaus stood on the 14th tee at Turnberry, waiting for the milling crowds to be cleared. Looking over at Nicklaus, Tom said: 'This is what it's all about.' 'Sure is,' said Jack.

Newspaper report

13. Reward for a Veteran
Jock MacVicar

I well remember Sunday, 10 July 1967. It was one of the most frustrating days I have ever endured as a golf writer.

To begin with, there was a newspaper strike in Scotland, a strike which was to last throughout the Open Championship at Hoylake later that week. There was always a ray of hope each morning that agreement would be reached. But by the middle of that afternoon the word from the office was: 'No chance of a paper tonight. But you'd better send a piece just in case.'

For a newspaper reporter nothing is more frustrating than having to write a story knowing it will never see the light of day; the same feeling, I reckon, as when you finish a medal round with two birdies after having torn up your card. It was with little enthusiasm, therefore, that I set off from my Hoylake guesthouse for the meeting of John Panton and Sam Snead at Wallasey.

With some 2000 spectators turning up to see the legendary Virginian, parking near the course was difficult. Eventually I found a spot in a side street and strolled in the warm sunshine to the first tee, my spirits rising with the temperature. I was going to enjoy this, paper or no paper. And John Panton might just surprise us by winning. Then I put my hand in my trouser pocket for a handkerchief: the car keys were missing.

I must have dropped them somewhere. Panic. The police? Yes, that was the answer: phone the police from the clubhouse, report the loss and pray that some Liverpudlian was not by then half-way to Manchester. There was nothing more I could do. Just settle down I told myself, listen to the larks and let Panton and Snead ease away the frustrations.

Amazingly, Panton and Snead did exactly that. At least Panton did. For this 36-hole match for the Teachers's World Matchplay title was to be John's finest hour.

Nobody gave him a chance. Here he was, fifty-one years of age with a fine record in British golf and in Europe, but nothing to compare with that of Samuel Jackson Snead, the man with the most gloriously rhythmic swing I have ever seen, except, perhaps, for those of Tony Lema and Jerry Pate.

Sam had been tenth in the US Masters earlier that year and by then had won more than a hundred events. He was four years Panton's senior – the same age as Ben Hogan and Byron Nelson – but still as supple as a twenty-year-old.

In fact, as he himself revealed on a later visit, Sam was double jointed. I remember him in the Longniddry clubhouse kicking so high that his toe touched the lintel of the lounge door. A photographer from the *Scotsman* was so intrigued by the performance that he asked, a touch diffidently – because Sam was not always the most approachable of men – if he would do it again for a picture. On this occasion Snead was delighted to oblige, and Jack Crombie got his picture, for which he received an award later in the year.

Anyway, this was the man Panton had to face over two rounds. The contrast between the two could hardly have been more striking. Snead had an arrogant walk, a straw hat and an inability to suffer men of ordinary talents gladly. A high handicapper once asked him how he was able to put stop on the ball.

'How far do you hit the ball?' asked Snead, impatiently.

'One hundred and twenty yards,' replied the hacker, by now biting his tongue.

'Then why the hell do you want to put stop on the ball!' barked Snead and moved off with imperious disdain.

Panton, on the other hand, would be dismayed by the thought of sending anyone away with a sore heart. Honest John is his nickname, and how accurate the description is. Scotland can never have had a better ambassador in the world of sport. I doubt if he has made one enemy in a career which began in 1935 and ended with his retirement in 1983 after thirty-seven years as club professional at Glenbervie.

He has never showed even a hint of arrogance. After he and Eric Brown tied for a tournament in the north of Scotland, officials wrestled with the problem of having two trophies, one large and ornate, the other small and plain. I recall how Panton duly walked out carrying – as we had forecast – the lesser trophy. Typical John.

Apart from a surprising liking for a flutter on the horses – his cap in one jacket pocket and the *Sporting Life* in the other was a common sight at tournaments – John was not a person to take chances. His hip pocket used to bulge not only with the current edition of the *Rules of Golf* but with previous editions as well, 'just in case'.

As the two men arrived on the first green at Wallasey, however, we immediately spotted an alarming weakness in the great Snead's armoury. His putting, which had deserted him some years previously, was now in such disarray that he had resorted to the 'sidewinder' method. He stood alongside the ball, toes pointing towards the hole, with his right hand down the shaft almost to the head of the putter. Aesthetically it was a disaster. Functionally, as it turned out, it was little better.

Panton, however, putted beautifully. I doubt if he ever putted better. And, quite against the odds, he was three up after four holes. Suddenly, the paper and the car keys seemed unimportant.

With the 6574-yard course playing short after weeks of sunshine, Snead's superior power was not a factor. No hole was out of reach in two, and the great American was looking uncomfortable, particularly on the greens.

But by the 13th the match was square. 'Here we go again,' we told each other. 'Another British player flattering to deceive.' But no! Who said golf was a predictable game? Three holes later John was three up again, and he completed the first eighteen holes still with that lead, having gone round in 69 to Snead's 73.

So our man lunched happily enough, though with not enough confidence to accept a glass of the sponsor's product. All he wanted was a cup of tea.

Indeed, for John it was always a cup of tea. I have even seen him quicken his pace at the prospect of a 'wee cup'. Some say they have actually seen him running, but I hesitate to go that far. Not that he was unathletic. John once played a trial for Hibernian Football Club before opting to follow the fairways rather than the roads to Ibrox, Parkhead and Pittodrie. It was just that his rhythm was steady, and the up-tempo of running might have ruined everything.

Early in the afternoon round Samuel Jackson Snead was sending out SOS signals. At the 28th he was five down, having watched, no doubt enviously, Panton hole two long putts on each of the first two greens. This was beginning to look a real story. But – oh, give me strength! – would there be a paper to print it in?

I hurried back to the clubhouse.

'Any chance of printing tonight?'

'Not a hope, son. But phone your copy anyway, so that we're covered.'

I returned to the course to find that Panton was now only seven holes from home and still five up. Then Snead birdied the 30th and 31st holes, leaving Panton only three up. Surely not, oh, surely not another British defeat snatched from the jaws of victory. . . .

Despair. John is bunkered at the 32nd, with his opponent safely on the green for a certain 4. This was all going wrong, as we had known it would. But wait! Panton is out of the bunker, and yes, yes – glory hallelujah! – he has holed the putt for a half. Three up and four to play.

But the Virginian is not finished yet. When he needs one most he produces a master-stroke at the short 34th with a long iron. The ball bounces on the front fringe of the green and rolls up only nine feet short of the flagstick.

These Yanks! Don't they ever know when they're beaten? How will Panton respond? After due consideration he pulls a 4-wood from his bag, takes a couple of practice swings, then gently wafts the ball through the still, warm air to within seven feet of the hole. A brave reply, achieved without fuss. No histrionics, no punching the air or saluting the crowd, which is not John's style.

But the real crunch had still to come. Now everything

depended upon sheer nerve. Technique was secondary. We said our prayers.

In the silence Snead had a careful look at the line of his putt and took up his awkward stance. Smoothly he stroked the ball. In it went, as we had feared, for a birdie 2.

Panton now had to hole his seven-footer for the match. If he missed it, then this World Seniors final was going to the 35th and probably beyond.

Again John showed no sign of the torture he must have been suffering. A brief look at the line, one practice stroke, and he was ready.

By now it wasn't just silence. It was a crowd holding its breath, a phenomenon to be experienced nowadays only on a golf course. We scarcely dared to watch as Panton's putter head moved slowly back, then slowly forward and through. The ball rolled forward, forward, forward – and suddenly disappeared. A great cheer erupted.

Honest John had made a half and won the match by 3 and 2. He was World Senior Champion.

Indeed, it was a day for honest men. For my car keys turned up at the local police station, having been handed in by an eagle-eyed passer-by, who had spotted them hanging from the lock on my car boot. On the day, I could claim a 2 and 1 victory – Panton and the keys against the absence of a paper in which to tell it all.

MEMO

> Grow old along with me!
> The best is yet to be
> The last of life, for which the first was made.
> *Robert Browning, Rabbi ben Ezra*

14. Slave of the Lamp

My first reaction to the sight of a golf course – so I am told – was to run away from it.

I was toddling along Machribeg shore, which runs parallel and to the right of the 3rd fairway at Dunaverty, when suddenly, without warning, I ran headlong into the Atlantic.

There was no explanation. There has never been an explanation, except, possibly, insanity. Just one mad moment at the age of three. Had it not been for prompt action by my father, who was then recovering from a serious illness, most certainly I would have perished. Clearly, my tendency to slice had taken hold even at a tender age.

I began to play golf in the evenings with my mother, around the five holes on the Machribeg side of the Conieglen burn. It always annoyed me that she was a better putter than I was, and the situation would become infuriating when, after calmly rolling in a putt, she would talk, going to the next tee, about the bacon and eggs we'd have for tea rather than about the relative pressures of the right and left hand on the putter grip. This approach to the serious business of golf was entirely beyond my comprehension, and, inevitably, I'd lose the next hole, though usually the game finished no worse for me than all square, possibly in the interests of peace.

Having been born and brought up no farther than a par 5 from the course, it never occurred to me to tackle any other game. My father played it, my uncles and cousins played it, and the regular summer visitors played it.

Clubs were handed down. Included in the set of 'plumber's tools' to which I fell heir was an astonishing implement that looked as if it had been found in a scrapyard. It was known as the 'wee black fella', a mashie with a darkly rusted head, a brown shaft, and a thin, shiny leather grip. It was as far removed from the gleaming technological products of today as an arrow from an Armalite. But it was deadly around the greens.

Superbly balanced, it served me marvellously. Shame at the sight of it, however, and the golfer's inability to resist the temptation to try something new, persuaded me to abandon it. This was a serious mistake.

The 'wee black fella' and an old hickory putter helped me to win the club's autumn meeting at the age of fifteen. But in truth my long game was a joke. Every drive was the same: high, short and sliced. I sought the assistance of the late Hector Thomson, then professional at nearby Machrihanish.

Old Hector was a lovely man. He was in his late seventies at the time, but he remained as erect as a guardsman, and he was a wonderful teacher. The Thomsons are all fine golfers. Old Hector's nephew is the famous Hector who won the Scottish Amateur Championship at St Andrews in 1935, the man who partnered Ben Hogan in the final round of the 1953 Open Championship at Carnoustie. His son, Arthur, is currently professional at Machrihanish, and his grandson, Peter, is at Erskine.

Like all the family, Old Hector was the most polite and charming of men. But he was not afraid to let you know what he thought of your method. After watching me wield a driver a couple of times, he fixed me with his eye and in his soft, lilting accent observed: 'Och, you would think you were using a scythe!'

Six lessons later Hector had my handicap down by five. It was a miracle, considering the material he had to work with. It was not so with Belle McCorkindale of Eden Farm in Southend. She was different.

Belle's family had never stepped on to a golf course. But, as with the rest of us, Dunaverty was near; and she had access to lush, green fields in which to whack away at grubby old golf balls. She rapidly came down to single figures, and by the time I was doing National Service with the Argylls at Bury St Edmunds and in Cyprus, she was on her way to becoming one of the finest women golfers this country has produced. She won every available prize at Dunaverty, except one. That was the Mixed Foursome competition in which she had the misfortune to have me as a partner.

We began steadily enough. But at the 3rd – yes, the one with the shore on the right-hand side – we took a 36. It is without doubt the highest figure Belle has ever had to write into a score card for one hole. To this day I aim off 45 degrees every time I set foot on that tee.

During 1958 I didn't play at all, spending the entire year in the foothills of the Troodos Mountains in Cyprus with 'C' Company of the Argylls. At the time the EOKA troubles were at their height. Our job was to root out terrorists, particularly the EOKA leader himself, Colonel Grivas. Luckily I had a 'cushy number'. I was the company clerk. Ordinarily, clerks and storemen rarely do any real soldiering. They are not required to do guard duty except in times of epidemic, and only the threat of a world war forces them to the indignity of actually having to carry a rifle.

But this man Grivas was escaping the net; and a time came when even the clerks and storemen were called out, the word being that the elusive colonel had finally been cornered.

Suddenly, the warm Mediterranean night was shattered by ear-splitting explosions. The blackness turned to blazing light. The rat was in the trap.

But where was the trap? And where was the rat? 'We sought him here, we sought him there, we sought him almost everywhere.' Turmoil continued for hours.

At the end of it Grivas was probably half-way to Greece, sipping his Keo wine and ready with another good yarn for his friend, Archbishop Makarios.

I am sure it was what happened that night that persuaded me to drop the lunatic idea of becoming a policeman. My interest in golf and in a soccer line-up that read Johnstone, Kilmarnock and Shaw, Cox, Paton and Redpath, Sloan, Humphries, Watson, Kelly and Aitkenhead – the great Motherwell team of the fifties – had me thinking about sports journalism. And not long after the abortive attempt to trap Grivas, Duncan McNicol, a feature writer with the *Glasgow*

Evening Citizen, arrived to do an article on the Jocks in Cyprus. My company commander, Captain Cookson, knew that I was interested in writing and kindly arranged that I should meet the man from the *Citizen*.

Less than a year later, and only a fortnight after being 'demobbed' at Stirling Castle, I was working in the *Citizen* office in Albion Street, Glasgow, having been taken on as a trainee sports writer with the *Scottish Daily Express*.

Those first few weeks were worse than National Service. At the time the *Express* was climbing to its peak in Scotland. There were so many people and so few chairs that for the first few days I could not even get a seat, let alone a typewriter. But the sports editor then was Bruce Swadel and he helped me to stick it out.

Among the many sports editors I have met over the years Bruce was the best. He was kind but firm, extremely knowledgeable – and not just about the great God soccer – and somehow he managed to handle a highly talented, if somewhat temperamental band of scribes and subs with rare skill. If a row was about to explode, Bruce would completely disarm his red-faced adversary with the words, 'Entirely my fault,' then put on his jacket and head downstairs to Tom's Bar for a large Bell's.

My first assignment was an international badminton tournament in Glasgow's Kelvin Hall. The evening proceeded predictably and without much excitement until suddenly, at ten o'clock, all the lights went out. In that moment my disenchantment with journalism vanished. Next morning I could scarcely believe it. They has used three paragraphs of my 'lights out' sensation. At last I was a sports writer.

Three years later, on the retirement of Jock Wemyss, I was offered the job of golf correspondent. My speed of acceptance then was faster than that of Nicklaus's driver-head as it strikes the ball. As if by a miracle my secret ambition had been realized. It all happened more than twenty years ago, and I can honestly say that at no time since then have I lusted after any other job on the paper.

It must be golf itself that produces so many marvellous people. It is a game of trust, a game in which you are on your own. You may try to deceive yourself, but deep down you know you cannot. Unlike the situation in soccer or rugby there is no one who can carry you through a game. Prima donnas are not encouraged. Cheats are abhorred.

Two years after being given the golf job on the *Express* I joined the Association of Golf Writers, a group formed at St Andrews in June, 1938, by about thirty journalists covering the Walker Cup. Bernard Darwin of *The Times* was its first president, and since then the Association has never been accused of failing to take itself seriously enough. To our colleagues in the rest of the newpaper industry we must seem like a cross between the Masons and a politburo. But we feel vulnerable. Who, in his right mind, would offer a job to an out-of-work golf writer?

Still, it is a comparatively healthy occupation in the unhealthy world of journalism, and if condensing ten hours of play at a golf tournament – some of which we have no chance of actually seeing – into 400 or 500 words is somewhat more difficult than putting together ninety minutes of a soccer match, we guard our jobs jealously. After all, we are out of the office for longer periods than any other member of the staff. Perhaps that is why the turnover among golf writers is considerably less than it is in other newspaper jobs.

It may also be the reason why so much warm comradeship exists in the AGW. We all know each other's faults, and we make fun of them, sometimes without mercy. But the good humour rarely spills over into bitterness. The knife in the back may be all too common in other areas of the newspaper business, but it is rare among the scribes who deal with golf.

Let me introduce you to some of the members. They won't mind a gentle jab or two; at least, I hope not. The glove is of velvet.

Take Renton Laidlaw. Does he own all the radio stations between Aberdeen and Abadan? If not, he must have a million shares in the microphone business. During the golf season the sun never sets on his honest voice. On one remarkable occasion, while doing his stint as a commentator on ITV, he was to be seen, during each commercial break, careering down the ladder from the control hut. In two minutes flat he would telephone a piece to Radio Scotland, career back up the ladder and be at his post again by the time the last advert faded off the screen.

Then there is my London colleague on the *Express*, Mark Wilson, the *Evening Standard*'s crack news reporter before sanity saved him. Mark must have been the model for Corporal ('permission to panic') Jones of *Dad's Army*. I have seen him on his knees in front of a television set pleading with the Almighty to deliver Tony Jacklin into the press tent as the tournament winner.

We also have Jacky Robertson of the *Glasgow Evening Times*. Jacky is one of our more peaceable members. Anyone can sigh or even sneeze on Jacky's backswing and he won't turn a hair. Preferably, however, he asks that you carry on your cacophony outside a 500-yard range.

Raymond Jacobs is deeply in love with the game as well. He is always an excellent read in the *Glasgow Herald*, but try to arrange a game with him and you just might have a problem. Raymond's idea of hell is to arrange a game, tentatively, put his trust in the Lord and an overnight monsoon, then open the curtains in the morning to a blazing sun and the realization that there is no honourable way out.

Perhaps our most peppery member is the *Daily Record's* Alister Nicol – or, as he is known to his best friends, the 'heat-seeking missile'. His eyes are perpetually ablaze, his mind tortured by the suspicion that somebody, somewhere, is plotting evil against the AGW. But of all of us he is perhaps the sharpest newshound, and 'blast him' - as my late grandfather, the Rev. Angus John MacVicar (the Padre) used to thunder – he is also the longest hitter of a golf ball.

Norman Mair, the former Scotland rugby international, will never win an award as one of Britain's snazziest dressers. But he has an elegant style with his pen, though its progress across the pages of his notebook is not renowned for rapidity. Had it not been for the fact that in his *Scotsman* days the first edition deadline was 9.30 a.m. assuredly he would have burned the midnight oil in the press tent. As it was, he munched through many a Mars bar in his quest after the right word.

Ian McNiven is the one who exclaims annoyingly, 'I've got the line!', when you are at your lowest ebb in the search for a good 'intro'. A thorough professional is Ian: not the trimmest of figures but a man of Olympic speed at the typewriter. He is also the best putter in our ranks. I doubt if even Tom Watson would get the better of McNiven on the greens. But then, Ian was once amateur champion of the Lothians.

Finally, in our gallop through the AGW *Who's Who*, there is Peter Dobereiner of the *Observer*, our plus handicap man in terms of writing ability. The 'Great Dane' once wrote scripts for *That was The Week That Was*; but golf eventually gobbled him up. There are those who ask why such a fine writer should be doing a job like this. Peter, however, is a man of simple tastes. Assure him of a glass or two of Mouton Cadet and he will make the description of a par 4 read like an entry for the Pulitzer Prize.

MEMO

. . . *tenet insanabile multos*
Scribendi cacoethes et aegro in corde senescit.
. . . an inveterate itch of writing, now incurable, clings to many,
                        and grows old in their distempered body.

Juvenal, Satires

15. 'What a Day for England!'

The 1971 Walker Cup match at St Andrews was a golf writer's dream: an occasion which, in my experience, has never been surpassed for drama, emotion and, finally, elation beyond belief.

We all arrived in the old grey town in late May and prepared to write our usual optimistic previews. No British and Irish side had beaten the Americans since 1938, but, even in the face of such bitter evidence, we could not write the lads off before the starting gun was fired. After all, this was the fiftieth anniversary of these transatlantic contests, and anyone with a sense of history – of symmetry, if you will – could not ignore the possibility of a result that for a generation amateur golf had been pining for.

Unfortunately, for me, the build-up to the contest was not as enjoyable as it might have been. I arrived in St Andrews with 'flu. On the eve of the tee-off I had the utmost difficulty in croaking out my story to a long-suffering copy-taker in Glasgow.

In the morning my throat was a little less painful. A few warming drams the previous evening had seen to that, though their quantity had not been sufficient to drown the feeling of foreboding as I walked out on to the course with my colleagues.

The British captain, Michael Bonallack, and the chairman of the selectors, Sandy Sinclair, had worked hard to instil in their men a strong team spirit, having picked the squad some months earlier and brought them to St Andrews nearly a week before the event. But the Americans, with Lanny Wadkins, Tom Kite, Vinny Giles and Steve Melnyk in their line-up, looked as formidable as any previous US team had done.

Incredibly, Britain won all four morning foursomes. But the backlash duly took place, the wounded Americans sweeping away with the afternoon singles, 6½–1½. The only British winner was that immensely likeable and highly talented man from Forres, Hugh Stuart.

Next morning the visitors tightened their grip on the match by capturing the second series of foursomes, 2½–1½. Now they were 9–7 in front, with eight singles to come on that final afternoon. We prepared to write another requiem, sad music for yet another British defeat after a glorious beginning. The staff in the Royal and Ancient clubhouse began to stack up the bottles of the Club's No 1 and No 2 whisky in the Big Room, ready for the ritual soothing of unhappy hearts.

Bonallack lost in the top singles to Wadkins. It was Bonallack's third defeat in four games, and, wisely, ever since then the home team has had a non-playing captain. Combining the pressures of playing with the strain of captaincy – morning, noon and well into the social evenings – is simply not on.

But now – out on the Old Course – things were beginning to stir. Stuart was winning again, this time by 2 and 1 over Giles. Warren Humphreys was rattling in two monstrous putts at the 15th and 16th on his way to a similar victory over Melnyk. Charlie Green was all square with one to play against Allen Miller. Charlie won the last hole with a solid par 4 and suddenly – we almost gasped for breath – the match was level.

Scoreboards reflected the turning of the tide, and as if by some telepathic process the whole of St Andrews began to gather around golf's most famous stage, Old Tom Morris's 18th green. Trade in the town that afternoon must have dropped almost to zero. They were four deep against the fences; they were leaning out of windows; they were craning necks out of skylights; they were perched precariously on the rooftops. Everyone seemed to sense that history was in the making.

It was about this time that the tall figure of the American non-playing captain, John Winters Jr., was seen trudging down the 18th fairway, over the bridge at the Swilcan and out on to the course. He was alone and forlorn as he searched for a glimpse of comfort on the scoreboards. There was none. Roddy Carr had just sunk a 30-footer across the 18th green to fell Jim Simons, and although Tom Kite had the beating of Geoff Marks, George McGregor and David Marsh were ahead.

McGregor, the only member of that team still a Walker Cup player twelve years later, edged home by one hole against Jim Gabrielsen. At almost the same moment, in his match with Bill Hyndman, David Marsh, the Southport doctor, was about to hit the shot of his life at the dreaded Road Hole.

Twice Marsh had to step away from his shot, first because of the cheering, rampaging spectators, then because of a man raking the Road bunker. David had a 3-iron in his hand. He knew it was the right club, and after a final practice swing, I heard him say out loud: 'Come on now, swing slow and watch the ball.' The ball came right out of the middle of the club. It soared gloriously into the air and thudded down in the middle of the menacing green 20 feet from the hole.

Marsh won the hole to go one up, then halved the 18th for a personal victory. In his dazed condition he had to be told at least three times by Bonallack that in gaining it he had also clinched victory for Britain in the Walker Cup.

Charlie Green recalls the joy among the players and gives his reasons for a rare victory. 'The team spirit was sky high. The guys all worked for each other, and the spectators were magnificent. The games were all going our way. The putts were going in and the shots made me feel it was more like a football match than a golf match. This was infectious, and it ran through the whole team and raised our games.'

As I walked back to the press tent to file one of the longest and most heart-felt reports I have ever written, I picked out a voice in the general tumult. It belonged to an elderly gentleman with a white moustache: an ex-army type.

'What a wonderful day for England!' he barked. 'What a wonderful day for England!' The hair at the back of my neck prickled. Considering the team had contained four Scots and an Irishman, I feel that the old boy ought to have suffered the same fate as the Scots caddy who had been working for the American team and had had the cheek to bet against the home side. Later that chaotic evening he was thrown into the Swilcan Burn, fully clothed.

Another reporting consignment which did nothing for my blood pressure was the Ryder Cup match at Royal Birkdale in 1969. This was a battle without parallel in the history of these confrontations between the best of the professionals in Britain and America. I can still feel the torture of suspense as it swung one way and then the other. And a lump still comes to my throat as I recall the final magnificent sporting gesture offered by Jack Nicklaus.

On the first day honours in the foursomes and the fourballs were shared 6 – 6. In the first series of singles the next morning Britain went in front 11 – 9, our Open Champion hero, Tony Jacklin, beating an out-of-touch Nicklaus by 4 and 3. This was the sort of performance Britain's non-playing captain, Eric Brown, had been looking for.

Eric, well nicknamed 'the Bomber', had made himself unpopular in certain quarters when, on the eve of the match, he had instructed his players not to search for any golf balls lost by their opponents. It was a shot of meanness across the bows of the Americans, and there are those who still snipe at Brown regarding his style of captaincy. But Eric has always been a battler. There is nothing sloppy or mealy-mouthed about him. Diplomacy comes second to a winning attitude in his list of priorities. It should not be forgotten that our three best results in the Ryder Cup were achieved under the captaincies of Brown, Dai Rees and Henry Cotton, fearsome men all in a 'crunch' situation.

Late on that final afternoon at Birkdale the hawk-like face of Brown was even more haggard with tension than usual. The match was swinging America's way, despite a fine 4 and 3 win over Lee Trevino by that redoubtable fighter, Bernard Gallacher. We needed 1½ points from Brian Huggett and Jacklin in the last two games to share the contest.

By then Jacklin and Nicklaus were approaching the 17th green, and Huggett and Billy Casper were on the 18th green.

Brown was dashing about, his hands thrust into his pockets in a vain attempt to look cool and casual. Nicklaus, one up at the time, hit the better shot on to the 17th, only a few yards behind the flagstick. Jacklin could only just get his ball on to the front ridge of the green, some 50 feet from the hole. The match was ebbing away from him. But then, to a roar which must have rocked Blackpool Tower, Tony sank his huge putt for a 3, and Nicklaus could not follow him in. All square.

Huggett, surveying a four-foot putt on the last green to halve his tie with Casper, thought that the mighty cheer signalled a Jacklin victory over Nicklaus and that now he had this four-footer to win the whole match. The gritty little Welshman holed it. He shook hands with Casper, then, mentally drained, collapsed into the arms of his captain. When, quietly, Eric told him that the match was not yet over, Celtic emotion overflowed.

It was an incongruous sight – a sobbing Huggett being consoled by his tough-looking captain, who at that moment must have had tears in his eyes as well.

By now it was nearly six o'clock, and Jacklin and Nicklaus were walking down the last fairway all square. They had both hit 3-woods from the tee, and anything could still happen for Britain in the Ryder Cup, a win, a defeat or even a draw.

Having comforted Huggett, Brown had hurried back down the fairway. He put his hand on Tony's shoulder. 'Are you nervous?' he said.

'Am I nervous?' said Jacklin. 'I'm petrified.'

'I just thought I'd ask you,' muttered Eric. 'If it's any consolation, I feel the same way.'

But the Open Champion kept his nerves under control. He struck a fine 8-iron to 30 feet from the 18th flagstick, only to see Nicklaus get to within 15 feet.

On to the green they came amid prolonged cheering.

'Come on, Jacko!' they shouted. 'You can do it.'

Eventually the hush. I felt as if I might never breathe again. At last Tony was ready. He stroked his putt. It looked good. It was going to be dead. No, damn it, it wasn't! It was two feet short: the length of putt nobody wants on the last green in a monthly medal, never mind the Ryder cup.

Nicklaus was bold. He went for the 'kill' from 15 feet, and overshot the hole by five feet. The tension was unbearable. The fate of the two most powerful golfing nations in the world depended on the sort of putts that make strong men quake.

Big Jack, carefully and methodically as ever, crouched over his ball, kept his head perfectly still and knocked the ball into the centre of the hole. Now Jacklin had this two-footer. What a tragedy, what an anticlimax if he missed! After the briefest of pauses, however, Jack bent down, picked up Tony's ball and handed it to him.

'I don't think you'd have missed it, but in the circumstances I would never give you the opportunity,' said Nicklaus as he offered his hand.

The match was over, a tie.

Rarely has one act of sportsmanship endeared itself so much to spectators. From that moment, Nicklaus, who had never quite been accepted as the natural successor to Arnold Palmer, was the hero. And remains so.

Writing later in his book, *The Price of Success*, Jacklin summed up his feelings thus: 'That was the only time I ever put pen to paper and wrote to another professional. I said, "Your gesture on the 18th green is something I'll never forget as long as I live." More than half of his team were bitching and going on about the fact that he gave me that putt. But Nicklaus plays the game in a spirit above the rest.'

MEMO

> Nor ever once ashamed
> So we be named
> Press-men; Slaves of the Lamp; Servants of Light.
>
> *Sir Edwin Arnold*

16. A Thin Red Line of Heroes

In a chapter mainly about heroes – and remembering that heroes do not always win – it would be unthinkable to leave out Gary Player. Pound for pound, Gary is the greatest golfing competitor who has ever lived. He is never more lethal than when he is down.

Some doubt his sincerity at times because of his insistence upon talking in glowing terms about players, courses, in fact anything that catches his fancy at any particular moment. But this is part of the Player philosophy of black and white. In his mind there are no greys.

The little man has never been more positive than in the 1965 semi-final of the World Matchplay Championship at Wentworth. It was a thirty-six-hole match and after eighteen holes he was six down to the American, Tony Lema, who, in the previous year, had won the Open Championship at St Andrews.

Lema had come home in 32 over the treacherous Burma Road, and Player looked a forlorn figure, particularly when he lost the first hole after lunch to go seven down with seventeen to play. This was surely the end for Gary against a thoroughbred like Lema. But the South African birdied the 2nd and 3rd holes to win both, halved the 4th with another birdie, and promptly birdied the short 5th as well to be only four down with thirteen holes to play.

When he missed a short putt on the 6th green, however, to slide five down again I was sure it was all over. The pendulum had swung back again. But Gary has never been one to follow an old script. He was determined to write a new one for himself.

He was still five down with nine to play. But he won the short 10th with a 3, then birdied the 11th. Three down with seven to play: Lema's beautiful swing was beginning to quicken ever so slightly. The 12th was halved. Then, at the 13th, the American hooked his drive, could only hack his second a few yards along the fairway and barely reached the edge of the green with his third.

After great deliberation, Lema holed his putt, from fully 30 feet, for a miraculous four. Now Player, on with two great woods, had to hole a ten-foot birdie putt to cut Lema's lead to two when only seconds earlier two putts would have been good enough. It was a curly putt, a nasty putt, but Gary gave it every ounce of concentration he possessed and in went the ball. Two down, with five to play.

The next two holes were halved, but at the 16th Lema snap-hooked his drive into the trees. One down, with two to play.

The 17th was halved with birdies, and so on to the 18th, with the light fading fast. Both hit good drives, but Lema was short with his second and Player slammed into a 4-wood, which he struck so hard that he almost swung himself off his feet. The ball, however, soared away with a slight draw and landed in the heart of the green, rolling to within ten feet of the flagstick. Gary reckons it was one of the best shots he has ever hit, and Lema failed to respond with a pitch and a putt. All square and on to the 37th.

Thousands of spectators, spellbound by the drama, charged towards the first fairway, anxious not to miss one second of this awesome struggle. The light was now almost gone, and it looked to me as if Lema, too, was almost gone, in a physical sense.

And indeed he was. Whereas Player found the green in two shots, Lema drew his second into a bunker and failed to get up and down to match his opponent's 4.

A match that is now a legend was over. Player sank to his knees on the edge of the green and wept. He told me later he had had a sudden vision of his farm near Johannesburg, his family, his farmhands, his horses, his home. It had inspired him. His resolute will to win had defied a mountain that had looked impossible to scale.

*

I have witnessed a great number of memorable moments in golf, both amateur and professional. Some were uplifting, others involved players in the crushing disappointment of having the prize whipped away in the cruellest of circumstances.

Two such occasions stand out especially for me: the 1970 Open Championship at St Andrews and the Open Championship two years later at Muirfield. Perhaps I did not quite appreciate it at the time, but in those two championships two strokes of a golf ball completely changed the lives of Doug Sanders and Tony Jacklin.

The scene at the 18th in the last round of the 1970 Open remains as clear in my mind as if it had happened yesterday. Thousands had gathered round the historic setting to witness Sanders edge out Jack Nicklaus for the most coveted title in golf. I had squatted down at the top of the clubhouse steps as the colourful Georgian prepared to play his second shot. Doug's personality was as sparkling as his attire. But this time I did not need binoculars to see the tension on his face. He required only a par 4 to beat Nicklaus, but in front of him was the Valley of Sin. I could almost hear him telling himself not to be short. Inevitably he was too strong, and the ball scampered up to the back of the green.

Nicklaus had no hope of getting a birdie 3. Sanders, therefore, had two putts for his first major title and lasting fame.

The downhill putt from the back of the 18th green at St Andrews is notoriously difficult to gauge for speed, and Sanders made the classic error. He left his first putt short by about three and a half feet.

The old grey town waited in silence. Sanders, his face now pale and drawn, hunched himself uncomfortably over his second putt. Suddenly, however, he stood up again, and picked an imaginary impediment from his line. The tension was killing him. It seemed that he couldn't bring himself to strike the putt that meant so much to him.

Finally, his concentration gone, he made contact. It was a diffident putt; his right hand came off the putter grip and the ball trundled to the right of the hole and remained above ground. Though he accepted the bitter disappointment with a dignity few others could have mustered and fought to within a stroke of Nicklaus in the play-off the following day, Sanders was never the same player again.

Two years later Tony Jacklin was within two holes of capturing the Open for a second time when his playing partner, Lee Trevino, perpetrated the most stunning – and the luckiest – shot I have ever seen in championship golf. It was lucky because, as Trevino admitted later, he had not given it his full concentration after bunkering his drive at the 17th, blasting his second shot out sideways, hitting his third into rough and his fourth over the green.

Meanwhile, Jacklin was not far short of the green in two and required only a pitch and two putts for a par 5, followed by a par at the last to beat Jack Nicklaus, who had charged in with a final round of 66. Tony elected to play a chip and run shot, expecting the ball to move quickly on the firm, fast green. But it didn't: it stopped 16 feet short of the hole.

Trevino, obviously angry with himself, then pulled a wedge quickly out of his bag, had a cursory glance at the flag and struck his chip from behind the green. To everyone's amazement the ball went straight into the hole.

'By tenfold that was the worst shock I've ever had on a golf course,' admitted Tony afterwards. Concentration ruined, he took three putts. The title had been snatched away from him.

It was a shattering mental blow from which he has never fully recovered. 'I went into a state of shock, and it definitely took me a long time to get over it, if I ever did get over it,' he admitted some years later.

In the autumn of that year Jacklin again found himself face to face with Trevino in the semi-final of the World Matchplay Championship at Wentworth. Tony was four down at lunch, but with a fine exhibition of precision golf, he hauled Lee back in the second round with an outward half of 29. He got round in 63 but still lost the match by a hole. Truly the talkative Texan was Jacklin's executioner.

If the Hollywood moguls had been there they would have bought the film rights of the 1977 Open Championship at Turnberry Hotel, the Open in which no one can ever remember who was third. This was a championship about two players. Tom Watson and Jack Nicklaus. They stalked each other for four rounds, through blistering heat and a thunderstorm. Neither gave an inch. All that was missing was John Wayne, a saloon bar and a musical score by Dimitri Tiomkin.

The final act, had it been scripted, would have been returned to the writer for being too corny, for having gone over the top. But it did happen, and Opens in the years that followed suffered by comparison.

I tipped Watson that year in the *Express*. In fact, half the press tent had put money on him, and so the final hour was doubly tense for us. After all, it was our chance to be right at last!

One shot, more than any other, won it for Watson. This was his putt of obscene length, up and down the hills and valleys of the short 14th, for a 2. When the ball vanished into the hole Nicklaus winced.

If it is possible to break Nicklaus, he was broken then, though he summoned up a miraculous birdie 3 at the last hole in a desperate attempt to catch the man whom he had always regarded the most likely to replace him. He was inches from destruction in the bushes after coming off his drive. But he found the green with his second and holed an enormous putt that owed more to his extraordinary will than to technique. Watson never looked like missing his tiddler, but in retrospect the 18-incher *was* in the missable range, considering the circumstances.

But even before the ball disappeared we in the press tent were congratulating ourselves for an all too rare success in the forecasting business. Next morning, when I caught up with Watson at Prestwick Airport on his way home to Kansas, he was wearing a large pair of dark glasses. Obviously, like ourselves, he had spent little of the night in bed.

MEMO

Given that he understands the game's customs and courtesies, the bad player can play with acceptance alongside the good, because golf so lends itself to handicapping.

Norman Mair

17. Courses and Characters

It is perhaps no coincidence that the most dramatic Open Championship of all took place at Turnberry Hotel's Ailsa Course. As any footballer will tell you, it is considerably more inspiring to play at Hampden Park than at Crewe, and an opera singer is much more likely to perform better at La Scala, Milan, than at the Beach Pavilion, Skegness. So I believe it is with golfers at Turnberry. There are few more compelling sights than that from the front steps of the hotel, looking down over that marvellous stretch of golfing country, with the Firth of Clyde, the forbidding hills of Arran and the stark dome of Ailsa Craig providing a Walt Disney backdrop.

It is difficult to believe, as you cast your eyes towards the dunes and the gorse, that here during World War II the course was bulldozed to bits for a Coastal Command air station. Portions of the 18-inch-thick concrete runways remain as a reminder of those grim years. Shortly after the war, however, the glory of Turnberry was restored by the Edinburgh-born golf course architect, Mackenzie Ross. Ross regarded Turnberry as possibly his finest work, though his genius can also be experienced at Southerness on the Solway Firth, at Estoril in Portugal and at Hardelot, a gem of a course in northern France, near Boulogne.

I remember Hardelot well, not only because it reminded me instantly of Rosemount, near Blairgowrie, but also because the club's kitchen staff produced the most delicious cold custard tart I have ever tasted.

It is every golfer's dream to play a course with excellently designed holes, fairly distributed bunkers and manicured greens. But a golf course without an inspiring setting is like a picture in black and white. On a bad day with the clubs, a beautiful course makes your walk worth while. On a day when the ball is soaring away sweetly from the centre of the clubface, the bonus of a gorgeous view elevates your soul to the 'gates o' Paradise'.

However, as with genius and madness, paradise and hell on the golf course are rarely far apart. I recall 1974 when the organizers, in their wisdom, decided to stage the John Player Classic at Turnberry during the time of the equinoctial gales. The savage winds ripped through the tented village, smashed scores of televisions sets, and, for the first time in my knowledge, rendered the press tent a 'no-go' area. Electric strip lighting crashed about our ears and workmen wearing crash helmets rushed in and out of the tent imploring us to leave as quickly as possible. All of us hastily took their advice – all of us, that is, except Norman Mair, the *Scotsman* correspondent, who, as always, was in a cocoon of concentration. He remained at his post, barking his copy down a sagging telephone line, totally unaware that a posthumous VC was only inches away.

That was Turnberry at its wildest, and when the wind blows at Turnberry there are few wilder spots betwixt the polar regions. But three years later the sun shone and the two greatest golfers in the world, Tom Watson and Jack Nicklaus, chose the Ailsa Course as their stage for an epic Open Championship finale.

Mind you, there are few more beautiful vistas than the one from the 10th green at Dunaverty, my home club. It is on a hill, which has been called Mount Zion, and there before you lies Dunaverty Rock, with the misty hills of Ulster on the horizon and a glistening strip of the Atlantic in between. If you are under par as well, the view becomes even more beautiful.

Mount Zion is the reason I am a links man. Seaside golf may not always be fair. But, while one parkland course is pretty much like another, each links course I have played has a character of its own. And, as Jack Nicklaus once remarked: 'Golf was never meant to be fair.' It is an astonishing fact, however, that few of Scotland's foremost golfers were brought up on the major links courses. John Panton came

from the heart of Perthshire, Eric Brown and Bernard
Gallacher from Bathgate, Ronnie Shade from Duddingston
and Charlie Green from Dumbarton. Links golfers may fairly
claim that the wind tends to rip their swings asunder. Perhaps
too many of us are carried away by the scenery to concentrate
on such mundane matters as a one-piece takeaway.

There are many great inland courses in Britain. Nearly all
of them have been constructed on heathland, like Sunningdale, the Berkshire, Wentworth and Walton Heath in the
home counties, Woodhall Spa near Lincoln, Hollinwell in
Nottinghamshire, Ganton in Yorkshire, and Rosemount and
Gleneagles in Scotland. Woodhall Spa is a particular
favourite of mine, partly because of its comparative remote-
ness. Why does it seldom feature in lists of the top-ranking
courses? Perhaps because it is rarely played by professionals
or seen by those of us who cover only professional events.

But back to the sea and another of my favourite courses:
Carnoustie. No one could possibly describe Carnoustie as a
gem, more a rough-hewn piece of granite – stark and, to the
cosseted parkland golfer, utterly forbidding. The finish is the
most feared in championship golf, with the Barry Burn
snaking hither and thither, ready to gobble up all but the most
accomplished and cool-headed players. It has a fearsome
collection of bunkers. One of them, at the 14th, was the scene
of some decidedly uncomfortable moments for Jim Hay, the
amateur from Kirkintilloch.

It happened in the 1967 Scottish Amateur Championship
when Jim took up his stance in the trap and discovered that
the piece of metal peeking out of the sand only a few inches
away was a bomb. Thinking it was only a smoke bomb, Jim
whacked the ball out and, fortunately, remained in one piece.
Later in the day, however, an officer from the army disposal
unit revealed that the object was a live mortar shell which
must have found its way into the bunker from the nearby
ranges. (It occurs to me that whoever fired it must, in the
gunnery sense, have been a 24-handicapper with a prodigious
slice.) The officer duly rendered the device harmless, but not
before he had brought it into the press tent and given us the
story. I am told that he was later court-martialled for this

cavalier behaviour. No doubt others may argue that his only mistake was in having missed a glorious opportunity to remove a section of the press at a stroke.

At Muirfield there are eighteen of the finest and fairest links holes in the world. But at the risk of incurring the wrath of the Honourable Company and its host of admirers, including Nicklaus, Muirfield, taken as a whole, is not to me the most inspiring of settings. It is an expert layout and a joy to play. But my heart leans more to the rocky shores of Turnberry, to the towering sand dunes of Royal Birkdale, and to the Mountains of Mourne at Newcastle, County Down.

It was at Newcastle in 1970, when it hosted the Amateur Championship, that most of us paid our last visit to Northern Ireland. Soon afterwards the 'troubles' swept away all regular international sporting links. But that was a marvellous occasion. The sun beat down all week – 'powerful wather' as the locals described it – and Michael Bonallack won his fifth and final title, thrashing his distinguished American opponent, Bill Hyndman, by 8 and 7. The Sleive Donard Hotel, at the time one of the best golfing hotels in the British Isles, again came up to expectations, especially in regard to the quality of its lemon meringue pie. Jacky Robertson of the *Evening Times* provided some offbeat entertainment by winning the Kilkeel Open, though when he rushed back to the hotel in the evening, with pride-filled eyes and empty pockets, we all had to fork out the cash to fill the handsome cup.

Jacky never did have the chance to defend his title. Not long afterwards I was saddened to hear that both the hotel and the local telephone exchange had been targets for the bombers. Instruments of destruction are difficult to imagine in such a tranquil setting.

Continuing the Irish theme, I recall a great character – no longer with us – among the ranks of the Belfast press corps. On occasions Jack was overtaken by an unquenchable desire to see the bottom of a bottle of Jameson's. Eventually one short-fused copytaker in his office decided that he had had enough and promised himself that the next time this particu-

lar reporter came on the line, obviously under the influence,
the plug would be pulled out on him. It was around this time
that the paper's editor asked Jack to help him with a speech he
had to make next day by furnishing the words of *McNamara's
Band*. Like the professional he was, Jack agreed at once but
explained that it might be some time before he could get the
words: they were in a book back at home across the city.
'Phone them in,' suggested the editor. An hour later Jack –
who had not stopped on his way even for a quick one
– telephoned his office and asked triumphantly for 'copy', no
doubt thinking about the bonus that might be his next time he
bumped into the editor.

'Jack here.'

'Oh, yes,' replied the tired, suspicious voice at the other
end. 'Fire away.'

'Me name is McNamara, I'm the leader of the band – '

'That's it!' roared the copytaker. 'Drunk again!' And
banged down the receiver.

I don't know if the editor ever did get his words, but the
story helps to illustrate the sometimes edgy relationship that
exists between a reporter and a copytaker. One of the most
important lessons that can be learned by a newspaperman is
never to fall out with a copytaker. If you do, and you are miles
from home, your only link with actual print is gone.

A quick, accurate copytaker is a key-figure in newspapers.
Sadly, with new technology, his days may be numbered. This
is a pity. Making contact with a human being at the other end
of a line, and hopefully having a friendly chat before getting
down to business, is so much more reassuring than punching
away at the direct input machine which all reporters in the
field will carry before the end of the century, possibly even of
this decade. New technology is sweeping through all kinds of
businesses and industry at such a pace that it occurs to me to
wonder what people will actually do in the twenty-first
century. As far as unemployment is concerned, we have not
seen the half of it yet.

Copytakers, for the moment at least, are an even more vital
link when you are abroad, though on many occasions the old
telex machine has proved to be of value. We had a particular-

ly good lady telex operator in the press room at the Hague Golf Club during the 1977 European Amateur Team Championship in Holland.

She spoke excellent English, got the stories over to the various offices quickly and efficiently and was always charming and polite. She was also pregnant and we decided to collect some guilders to help her buy something for the baby. This was duly done. But when the day came to hand them over a frenzied Irish journalist rushed up to us on the course, eyes bulging, and exclaimed: 'I hope nobody has given that girl the money yet. We can't start pushing guilders into her hand as if she was some poor soul. Do you know who she is? A niece of the Queen of the Netherlands!'

So we never did thank our telex operator in guilders. In retrospect, I think we should have done. She was not the type who would have taken our gesture amiss.

Two years later we were in Denmark for the same championship at a comparatively new course outside the busy fishing port of Esbjerg. Esbjerg was notable for two things, the coldest first day of July I have ever experienced and what must surely be the most crazily contoured green in existence. It is built on the side of a hillock, with the hole cut right at the top of a sharp slope. Joe Carr stood there for hours taking bets against players getting down in four putts. He won a small fortune.

Mention of a golf green brings me to one of my pet subjects: course watering. In recent years many clubs have had water specially laid on, at considerable expense in many instances, and in their desire to justify the outlay have ruined the greens they were so keen to improve. Too many greenkeepers and greens conveners seem to think they must make the most of the facility and forget that except in a real drought ten minutes of light watering in the evening is more than sufficient. Enthusiasm for the hose and the pop-up sprinkler has produced more thatch and moss on greens in a few short years than nature did in generations.

On the subject of course construction and maintenance, I should like to mention two more of my *bêtes noires*: blind second shots at medium-length par-4s and uphill opening holes. Blind tee-shots I can live with, but since the essence of good iron play is accuracy, surely the player has the right to see his target, the flagstick. As for uphill first holes, they fill me with foreboding. I cannot imagine a less encouraging way to set out upon a round of golf.

The Old Course at St Andrews is, of course, riddled with holes where blind and semi-blind shots have to be played. So is Prestwick. But they are originals. The first written evidence of the existence of the Royal and Ancient Club at St Andrews is dated 1754; and although twenty-three clubs were in existence before it was founded in 1851 Prestwick is the cradle of the Open Championship. Twelve championships were held there before St Andrews was first used in 1872.

Both courses are so heavy with atmosphere that you can almost see Willie Park, Tom Morris, J.H.Taylor and Harry Vardon striding the links in their waistcoats and tweed jackets, carrying their hickory clubs under their arms and crouching over their gutta-percha golf balls. The Open Championship has progressed from eight entrants at Prestwick in 1860 to more than a thousand in the 1980s; but at St Andrews and Prestwick history is paramount and must never be destroyed by the bulldozer and the march of time. It would be a sorrowful day, for example, were the gingerbread, the Stilton and the vintage port to disappear from the Prestwick clubhouse. And where else would you discover the notice in its changing rooms: 'Do not throw your cigar butts in the urinals.'

Speaking of Harry Vardon, what would he have made of Ken Brown, that talented but troubled young Scot from Harpenden? Vardon was so serene that he played, according to Horace Hutchinson, 'with a certain gay and gallant courage'. Brown, alas, bottles up so much emotion within himself that he does not, in my opinion, do himself anything like justice. The pent-up pressure manifests itself in many ways. He has been fined regularly by the PGA, and he rarely talks to the press, even on occasions actually running away from a man with a notebook and pencil.

If Ken would only relax and smell the flowers – as he tried gallantly to do when he found himself partnering myself and two other journalists in the pro-am prior to the 1982 Haig Tournament Players' Championship at Hollinwell – I am sure he would be a regular winner. He has all the shots.

He should take as an exemplar Jack Nicklaus, who says that the very reason a golfer turns professional is to get into the pressure position of winning tournaments. Defeat is not the end of the world if you have given your best. I remember that great Argentinian, Roberto de Vicenzo, marching into the press tent, after losing an Open, and enquiring of the assembled ranks of serious-faced journalists: 'Why are you so sad?' Within seconds Roberto had everybody smiling. And again Jack Nicklaus: 'If you lose you don't feel all that good inside. But if you have given it your best shots, you put a smile on your face, stick out your hand and say, Well done!'

Within that quote is the very essence of golf and the way it should be played. Hopefully, it will continue to be played like that by most people, even if the game is big business in many quarters nowadays and has spread to every corner of the globe from this small island.

The game is now a fever in Japan. It was first played there seventy-five years ago; but 'gorufu' did not rise like the sun until the age of Arnold Palmer in the fifties and sixties. Today it is estimated there are ten million golfers in Japan. Vast numbers of them have never even seen a golf course. They thrash away – seemingly caught by the bug which you and I always thought lurked only amid gorse and dune – in two- and three-tiered driving ranges.

Club golf, as we know it, is only for the wealthy. Membership fees range from £6000 to a staggering £175,000. Public courses are few, and even if you are lucky enough to procure a teeing-off time you will'pay in the region of £15 for a round on weekdays and £30 at weekends.

Golf is also a major sport and business in Australia, New Zealand, Africa and Far East countries like Thailand, Malaysia and the Philippines. The game can also be found, surprisingly, on the 38th Parallel, at Panmunjon in Korea. There is only one green and only four tees, and these are periously close to a minefield between North and South Korea. An unlikely setting. But it proves the psychological qualities of golf. It was built to provide the UN peace-keeping forces with a facility to relieve the tension and the boredom.

There is also another course at Kathmandu, another in the shadow of the pyramids in Egypt and a nine-hole layout at Bucharest in Rumania. Planning has also gone into the construction of Russia's first course near Moscow.

King James IV really did start something when in 1502 he bought clubs and balls from a bowmaker in Perth so that he could retreat for an hour or two from trying to rule a nation of Scots who, at the time, were more concerned with less gentlemanly pursuits than a game of golf.

I now hand back to my father, who proposes to write a chapter on putting: a chapter which he insists will be useful to students of the game. Knowing the quality of his putting, I suspect that the exercise may be compared with the efforts of a cripple to teach an innocent child to walk. On the other hand, Beethoven was stone deaf, and he wrote some inspiring music.

MEMO

The game is ancient; and kings have played it. Its origin is obviously aristocratic. At the same time, in its sustained growth, it has kept step with the democratic trend of our institutions and has touched the further extreme in its general adoption by all classes. What the future may hold in store for its fortunes it is impossible to foretell; but of one thing we may be fairly certain. In any future history of the social life of our times, the game will not be left out of the picture.

Roger and Joyce Wethered

The practice ground at the Mull of Kintyre, *c.* 1910

Ugadale Arms Hotel, Machrihanish, *c.* 1930. It was over this hotel that
Jimmy Lyon from Dunaverty drove a 'gutty' from the face of a watch (see
page 65)

Matchplay champion: John Panton is presented with the *News of the World* trophy at Hoylake, 1956. The finalist, Harry Weetman, is seated left

A conquering hero to his public at Scunthorpe. Tony Jacklin's return to his home town after winning the Open at Royal Lytham, 1969

A conquering hero to his family. Tony Jacklin with his wife and parents after
his victory at Royal Lytham

High Kicker: Sam Snead (at sixty) demonstrates his suppleness. Dai Rees
looks on in amazement in the background

Above left: 'I've done it again!'
Tom Watson winning the Open at
Muirfield, 1980, with caddie Alfie
Fyles

Left: The honorary Scot. Tom
Watson once again, after winning
his fourth Open, all played in
Scotland (Carnoustie, Turnberry,
Muirfield and Troon)

Public Relations: Jimmie Letters, managing director of John Litters, late of Hillington, Glasgow, with John Panton, Cathie Panton and Lee Trevino

'I was moving in exalted company, so I put on my best suit!' Jock, with Ian McColl, formerly the editor of the *Daily Express*, and Severiano Ballesteros

'Watch out! I'm going to be a golfer like by dad!' Sandy Lyle (aged four) with his father, Alex Lyle, at Hawkestone Park

'I like scrambling — on the course and on my bike!' Sandy Lyle

Making peace with the press. Ken Brown, with (left to right), Mike Britten,
Exchange Telegraph; Jock, *Daily Express* and Bill Elliot, *Daily Star*

'Blast!'

18. The Black Yips

As Jock implies, my putting has for some time been a matter
for levity among fellow members at Dunaverty. I can neither
'drive for show' (principally on account of waning suppleness)
nor 'putt for dough', though with a 4-iron down to a
pitching-wedge I believe I can still hold my own with anybody
over the age of seventy. That is not to say, however, that I
have failed to study the art of putting. In fact, even as this is
being written a corner of my brain is busy analysing a new
method which may lead me to perform astonishing deeds
when I have mastered it. (Later in the chapter I will describe
it, in shy detail.)

My father (the Padre) never believed in the old adage,
'Practise what you preach.' His advice to his parishioners was
more sophisticated: 'Don't do as I do, do as I say!' If I had a
drink problem (which, fortunately, I do not have, due to no
personal merit but entirely to my chemical make-up) I would
rather look for guidance from an alcoholic than from an
innocent teetotaller. Arguing along such lines, I believe that
what I have to say about putting may be found useful by
fellow sufferers. On the other hand, if you are a good putter,
then perhaps you ought to take Jock's implied advice and
read no farther, in case of infection. 'Out, damned spot!' said
Lady Macbeth. 'Hell is murky!'

In my young days I was a competent putter; at times,
indeed, inspired. I remember winning a monthly medal by
sinking a 30-foot putt across the 18th green, in full view of the
crowded clubhouse windows. This is as fragrant and valuable
a memory to me as his long putt to win the Open at Troon in
1962 is to Palmer, all happiness being relative to an individual's life-style or golfing ability. But I can scarcely bear to

describe what would happen to me now, some thirty years later, in the unlikely event of my having the same length of putt to win a medal, especially with the faces of my 'friends' leering from vantage places in the clubhouse.

Whereas, on that distant day, I stood firm and straight and steady, nerves well under control, now I might crouch over the ball with contorted limbs, nerves twitching like the tappets in an engine. Whereas, on that distant day, I took the putter-head smoothly back and followed through with in-souciant grace, now, after long travail of spirit, I might utter a soundless scream of agony, jerk and stab at the ball and, probably after hitting it twice, send it scuttering in a direction bearing no relation to the hole. No medal. No handshakes. No smug and falsely modest reference to a 'flukey one' as I enter the clubhouse. Only semi-hysterical laughter to camouflage pain and a repetition of Tommy Armour's ghastly joke: 'Once you've had 'em, boys, you've got 'em.'

My partner might try to comfort me by re-telling Bobby Jones's story about 'Wild Bill' Mellhorn, one of America's foremost professionals between the wars, who, finding his approach only three feet from the hole, lunged at the ball so desperately that it shot across the green into a bunker. But there would be no comfort in the story. I am only too well aware that after his traumatic experience 'Wild Bill' never played competitive golf again. And I have no desire at all to give up competitive golf. Indeed, I approach every game with the hope that my Creator will suddenly smile and whisper in my ear: 'You have suffered enough, my son. Today the yips will entirely vanish and you will be a good putter again.' (How long, O Lord, how long?)

In the 'corridors of the ages', when I could putt, it never occurred to me to consult books on the subject. I simply held the club comfortably and naturally and swung its head easily through the ball. If the ball went into the hole, well and good. If it did not, then it was because of a hidden slope on the green or a worm that had cast up earth in the wrong place. It was never my fault that I missed. I had full confidence in the rectitude of my 'method'. Indeed, I was unaware that I did have a 'method'.

The years passed. During a spell when I was missing putts more often than usual – an inevitable spell in every golfer's experience – I began to study what the top professionals had to say on the subject. It was a mistake. From then on my confidence was eroded, deteriorating like a rusty car to a stage of almost complete collapse.

My decline and fall began with the realization that every 'master' who has written about putting has a method which is strictly his (or her) own.

For example, Roger and Joyce Wethered advised: 'Do not think of following through.' Bobby Locke wrote: 'Concentrate on following through as far as the putter goes back in the backswing.'

Bobby Jones said: 'Take plenty of time to get your breathing and heart tranquilized.' 'Miss 'em quick,' growled George Duncan, an exhortation that was to be repeated, years later, by Babe Zaharias.

'Never hit a putt with the heel of the club,' insisted Locke, 'because that puts check on the ball, and it will not run as far as you expect.' Seve Ballesteros declares that he strikes the ball near the heel of his putter 'to see that it stays square'. 'Keep your weight mostly on your left foot,' writes Don Herold. Mark Harris, an American golfer for whom, curiously, Herold says he has a deep admiration, takes the view that 'your weight should be evenly distributed'.

Claude Harmon, the American professional, once said that 'a good putter can be made'. Peter Dobereiner believes that 'putting is such an individual matter that it is impossible to lay down dogmatic rules'. I am now inclined to agree with Dobereiner. But such a negative statement was of no great assistance in my search for truth.

Perhaps the most positive and helpful hint about putting that I have come across in a book was offered not by a champion golfer but by a champion golfer's wife. One evening in their hotel, during an important tournament, Ben Hogan was complaining to his wife about his putting.

'Would you like to know how to sink those putts?' she asked.

'You know how?' Hogan said.

'Yes, I do.'

'Then why the hell haven't you told me? How?'

'Just hit the ball a little nearer the hole,' said Valerie.

The logic of it is breathtaking. It affected me like a flare of sunshine in the midst of a rainstorm, and for a time I putted better. But soon, as I continued to read instructional books and watch professionals at work on the greens, confusion returned.

Bobby Locke putted off the left foot, with a closed stance. So did Eric Brown. Roberto de Vicenzo putted off the right foot, with an open stance. So, at times, did John Panton. Arnold Palmer putted from dead centre, with a square stance. So does Seve Ballesteros. Jack Nicklaus crouches over the ball. Tom Weiskopf stands straight. Isao Aoki, from Japan, perhaps the most successful putter of them all, addresses the ball with the toe of his putter pointing heavenwards, apparently in defiance of the laws of nature.

Doggedly I tried all those methods, one by one. I rapped the ball with firm wrists and did not think about following through. I stroked the ball with supple wrists and determinedly followed through. I putted off my left foot. I putted off my right. I struck the ball near the heel of the club. I struck it off the toe. I crouched. I stood straight. I leant forward on my left leg. I leant back on my right. I bent forward with straight arms until the toe of the putter pointed to the sky, like Isao Aoki's. But I still could not putt. Rather did I begin to suspect that all the physical stress involved in such experiments might be the cause of the rheumatic twinges now occurring in my elbows and right hip.

In the end it dawned upon my woolly and unscientific mind that since all those 'masters' were – and are – good putters, their varied styles and apparently contradictory advice must surely contain some common denominator. After long study I found it. 'Keep your eye on the back of the ball, your head and body perfectly still at impact.' It was like a revelation from on high.

Jean, my wife, has always been a good putter. At one stage, before the slipped disc put an end to her competitive days, she won several putting prizes in a row and I made the suggestion that she ought to turn professional and put up a notice at Achnamara front gate: 'Putting Taught Here.' She was not amused. Nor was she particularly impressed when I told her about my 'revelation'.

'Keep your eye on the ball and remain still at impact?' she said. 'Everybody knows that!'

'Well, I haven't been doing it,' I said.

'That's why you can't putt.'

Valerie Hogan and Jean MacVicar: sisters under the skin. I knew then how Ben must have felt when faced with his wife's simple logic. Like murder.

But I put aside inhuman emotions. I went out on to the course and began to practise putting with new hope. And as I held my putter in a way that felt natural – albeit with the 'over forty' forefinger of my right hand pointed down the shaft – and swung it naturally at the ball, without moving head or body, I was amazed – and made instantly euphoric – by the results.

I remembered an obscure pamphlet I had once read, prepared by William B. Langford, an American golf-course consultant, which indicated the quality of putting required from champions. I went home, rummaged like a frenzied mole in my disorganized filing system, found the pamphlet and consulted the simple table it contained.

With putts of from 1 to 3 feet a champion ought to sink 9 out of 10; from 3 to 5 feet, 8 out of 10; from 5 to 7 feet, 7 out of 10; from 7 to 9 feet, 6 out of 10; from 9 to 11 feet, 5 out of 10; from 11 to 13 feet, 4 out of 10; from 13 to 15 feet, 3 out of 10; from 15 to 17 feet, 2 out of 10; and from 17 to 24 feet, 1 out of 10.

From a distance of 1 to 3 feet I had indeed been sinking 9 putts out of 10 and from 3 to 5 feet, 8 out of 10. I gave thanks to my Creator: I had the quality of a champion. During the following days and weeks – as I remembered to keep head and body still – my confidence built up like red-hot lava within a volcano. I won two monthly medals in a row. (Sceptics seeking verification of this statement are invited to consult the Dunaverty records for January and February 1981.)

'Who's the one to give putting lessons now?' I said to Jean.

She merely smiled. Was there a trace of pity in that smile?

Then one day it happened. The occasion was a hard-fought four-ball with Jim McPhee against Boskers and Big Allan. I had a four-foot putt to win the game on the 18th green. In my eagerness to get the ball into the hole I forgot, for the fraction of a second, the great truth about stillness. I swayed forward on the putt, realized the mistake immediately and jerked my head back and the club-head forward in an effort to counteract it. In a blur of mental pain I saw the ball shoot six feet past the hole.

I felt as an ancestor of mine at the Mull of Kintyre must have felt in the plague year of 1648 when he saw the first blotch on his body and realized that he had contracted the Black Death. I had contracted the Black Yips. The bubbling lava of confidence burst out of the volcano and flowed away, to become a grey, congealing mass of hopelessness.

In an effort to follow the advice that had helped me in my spell of putting health – 'keep the head and body still' – and, at the same time, to prevent the sway forward which is the genesis of the yip, I tried various stances. Upright like a pillar of salt, feet together, arms swinging pendulum-wise. Bent almost double, feet splayed wide (like Michael Bonallack), hands half-way down the shaft. Left toe almost touching the ball (like Neil Coles). Right toe almost touching the ball and stance so wide that it threatened trouble to the spine. All in vain. I still yipped.

The disease progressed. Ultimately it took so bizarre a turn that my companions were in the habit, as I prepared to putt, of moving away and contemplating the distant hills. The symptoms occurred only on putts of about a yard down to six inches. With steely resolution I would gaze down at the ball. 'Head still, body still,' I would tell myself. 'Slow back, slow forward and – ' At this point, with the putter-head approaching the ball, a spasm of terror would pass through my body like an electric shock. I would jump several inches in the air. Darkness would cover my eyes. When my sight cleared the ball would be far beyond the hole and I would be shaking, almost sweating. The day Jock let loose a howl of laughter, as he watched, I understood why the others turned away.

Non-golfers – and, indeed, golfers not affected by the yips – may look upon the above as a humorous exaggeration. They can be assured it is as coldly factual as any case-history published in the *Lancet*.

But how to find a cure? I loved my golf. On contracting the yips Henry Longhurst put his clubs away in an attic and gave up the game. I refused to take so defeatist an attitude.

I had a word with a friend who is a psychiatrist. Having listened to the tale of my symptoms he smiled with tolerance. 'A common trauma in my line of business,' he said. 'You are simply afraid of being afraid.'

'That's a diagnosis,' I said. 'It's a cure I'm after.'

'Well' – he hesitated – 'that's entirely up to yourself.'

'I'll do anything,' I said.

'Rid yourself of fear.'

'But how?'

'What about prayer?' He was laughing.

I have always suspected that psychiatrists are no earthly good to anybody. This one was certainly no good to me. Like everybody else he just laughed. He knew nothing about golf. But I took to heart one thing he had said. The cure, it seemed, was up to myself.

I began by experimenting with putters. For years I had played with a 'Wee Benny', a Sayers product with an orthodox blade and without too much rake on the steel shaft. Now I laid it aside and flirted with other models. I had no idea so many were available.

In spite of his superior attitude to my putting, Jock does not seem to have any greater confidence in his own, if the number of putters he uses is any guide. At one stage he had thirteen, of various shapes and sizes. Being a golf writer, he has the duty of keeping up to date with every new development in club design, and I suppose he is open to temptation while listening to smart salesmen describing the magic quality in each of their new products. His present favourite is a Japanese creation, which looks like something I might have made from Meccano in a bygone age. It operates well for him.

From Jock – and from other sympathizers – I borrowed a selection of weird instruments. Things like branding-irons.

Things twisted and curved like discards from the old bow-maker's shop in Perth which had a king for a customer. Things which went *ping*, and things which went *pong*. Things with tiny blades, and things with blades so large that they could have been used to drive in fencing-posts. Things with hickory shafts, steel shafts, carbon shafts, wooden heads and brass heads. Things with the shaft rising straight from the centre of the blade, and wry-necked models which made you stand so far away from the ball that you felt like a fisherman with a rod and line.

Fortunately, at the time, Gene Littler's new putter had not yet come upon the market. This has to be seen to be believed. A 'wrong-way-round' model, the blade points back from the shaft towards the player's body. The makers claim that such an arrangement keeps the face of the club flush with the ball at impact. I have a notion that if someone had offered me the Littler club at the height of my trouble, my mind, already boggled, might have fused altogether, like an electric plug with positive and negative wires transposed.

None of the putters I tried made any difference. By the exercise of immense willpower I was able to keep the yips at bay during 'friendly' four-balls. But when it came to scoring in a medal round the dreadful paroxysms would return whenever I was faced with a put of anything under five feet.

'It's all in the mind,' said Jock one day. 'Try to realize that even if you miss a putt it's not the end of the world.'

I took a deep breath and faced the truth. Salvation was not to be found in putters. I went back to my 'Wee Benny'.

Are the yips infectious? I put the question seriously, because before they took hold of me they had been torturing Big Allan, and for long periods I was exposed to the sight of his agonies. It must be admitted, however, that I watched those agonies with an amusement which I now acknowledge was shameless. Perhaps the simple answer is that my Creator decided to punish me for lack of proper sympathy with a fellow human being.

In any case, a time came when Big Allan and I suffered together. But then, after a holiday with his elder son at a distant course, he returned to Dunaverty with a glow of joy on his face. While away, he had practised Sam Snead's 'side-winder' method and it had cured his yips. (Strangely enough, from that day to this, no trace of the disease has been apparent in his golf – except perhaps in the matter of short chips.)

Inspired by a spirit of envy, I began working on my own 'method', chiefly from a psychological angle. After making a few experiments I decided that the 'sidewinder' was not for me.

But one day, by chance, I took up a fairly wide crouching stance, with my left foot well towards the hole to prevent sway and with most of my weight on it. The ball was mid-way between my feet and immediately below my head. Suddenly I felt comfortable and relaxed. I remembered what Jock had said about a missed putt not being the end of the world. I remembered that the day was fine and that I was striking my irons with authority and grace. My partner and opponents were all nice people; the salt of the earth, in fact. High in the blue a lark was singing, and I could actually feel the scent of the wild thyme. I had written a thousand words that morning which were not all bad. Jean had promised me a tasty curry on my return home. All in all, the world was fair and bright.

'A putt?' I said to myself. 'What the hell!'

I moved the blade back, paused, then moved it forward with careless ease, but with Harry Vardon's advice to Tommy Armour still clear in my mind: 'If you don't move your head, you won't move your body off balance and you've got to hit with your hands.'

The ball clunked as it struck the back of the hole and stayed in.

Life is meant to be happy, and a missed putt is but a tiny wrinkle on the graph of time, irrelevant to the fate of your immortal soul. Such a philosophy, I submit, is a prescription which may well be a cure for the Black Yips. For some time I have been free of them.

At any rate, the violent, jumping symptoms of the disease have not recurred, thanks, I believe, in part to that firmly planted weighted left foot and in part to a more positively cheerful attitude.But I know only too well that the virus still lurks in my blood, like the virus of the stammer I used to have as a boy, ready at any sign of irresolution to leap out, gibbering.

Those of you who do not play golf – and even some of you who do – may wonder why I love the game so much when it causes me a deal of pain in both mind and body. The question is complex and would require the combined skills of Burns, Shakespeare and P.G. Wodehouse to provide a comprehensive answer. Such an answer would treat of fresh air, exercise, beautiful scenery, good companionship, pride in achievement and the sublimation of aggression. It would deal with the vicissitudes of life and the love of a man for a maid. Life can be cruel, but in the widest sense it is exciting and ours to enjoy. A maid can be fickle and hurtful, but if she is your girl then nothing can change your love for her.

And putting, remember, is only a part of golf: an important part but not the be-all and end-all of the game. It has to be understood that if sometimes you miss a putt it does not necessarily mean you are a weakling or a coward or a failure in your business or profession. It simply means that you have missed a putt, and every golfer misses a putt, sooner or later. Cotton did it. So do Nicklaus and Watson and Greg Norman. And so – to the anguish of all who watch – does Bernhard Langer.

Bernhard was afflicted by the Black Yips at a surprisingly early age. But in this gallant golfer from Germany we have an example of a man who has come to terms with the disease and continues to play wonderful golf. He misses many short putts, but, to outward appearance, he does not allow this to annoy him and affect the rest of his game. He retains a smile.

There is a clergyman in America who, in the midst of a bout of the Black Yips, went to his Bible (1 Corinthians, 13) and, at a club dinner, produced this masterpiece of despair.

> Though I speak with the tongues of Palmers and of Hogans, and cannot putt, I am become as sounding brass and a tinkling cymbal.
>
> And though I have the gift of long drives, and understand all slices, and all hooks, and though

I have chips to remove mountains, and cannot putt,
I am nothing.

And though I bestow all my money to feed my family,
and though I give my body to be spurned, and cannot
putt, it profiteth me nothing.

Putts come long, and are very tricky. Putts envieth
not, putts vaunteth not themselves, are not puffed up.
They do behave unseemly, seeketh not the hole, are not
easily involved, thinketh nothing.

Putts never faileth. But whether there be golfers,
they shall fail; whether there be lies, they shall cease;
whether there be the know-how, it shall vanish away.

For now we know in part, and we putt in part. But when
that which is perfect shall come, then that which is in
putting shall be done away.

When I was a beginner, I spake with authority. I
understood as a beginner, I thought as a beginner; but
when I became a man I lost faith in my putter.

For now we see through a green darkly, but then
face to face. Now I know I cannot putt, and what
I know is also known.

And now abideth drives, chips, putts, these three:
but the greatest of these is putts.

How well I understand the feelings of this golfing clergyman, especially those which prompted the lines: 'Now I know
I cannot putt, *and what I know is also known.*' I, too, have
seen the smirk, the sudden turn away, the heaving shoulders
of my opponents. And in his unusual scripture exercise I
recognize a plea to his Creator for succour and guidance.

Having grovelled in the mire, was he at last vouchsafed the
understanding that he could be a happy golfer without being
an expert putter? I like to think so.

The great paradox of the game – at least in my experience –
is that when you wipe the dark glass clear and admit to
yourself that you cannot putt, you become at once a better
putter. And faith and hope return.

MEMOS

> Wee sleekit, cow'rin', tim'rous beastie,
> O what a panic's in thy breastie!
> > *Robert Burns, To a Mouse*

> O wad some Pow'r the giftie gie us
> To see oursels as others see us!
> It wad frae mony a blunder free us,
> > And foolish notion.
> > *Robert Burns, To a Louse*

19. At the 19th Hole

It is doubtful if any golfer, at the end of a round, feels entirely satisfied with his performance. Here and there, along the way, there have been missed putts, fluffed chips, skimmed iron shots and hooky drives, each a scar on the smooth surface of desired perfection. Having completed the round of this book, Jock and I have the same vague feelings of dissatisfaction.

We sit in the best clubhouse in the world, looking out along the length of the 18th fairway, with the sea and the Rock of Dunaverty in the background, watching a four-ball moving erratically towards the home green. There is a nip in the air outside and, being slightly tired, we take restorative sips of a superb whisky distilled from grain grown on Boskers's farm. (It is called Old Machrimore – after the farm – and cannot be bought in any pub or shop.) We admit that we have played reasonably well but that many opportunities were missed.

The purpose of our round was to convey to others the essence and flavour of golf and the many causes of our love for it. We realize, however, that though we tried hard several faults occurred in our play.

For example, we did not deal with denigrators of the game, such as Michael Parkinson, who once said: 'Golf is a bore, a drag, a 24-carat yawn. As a game to be played it comes bottom of my list, somewhere between clay-pigeon shooting and underwater cyclo-cross, and as a spectator sport it hardly registers.'

Poor Michael. He used to broadcast with verve and style about sport in general and football and cricket in particular; but when the likes of George Best and Freddie Truman departed and Peter Alliss came on the scene to describe the spectacular deeds of Nicklaus, Neil Coles, Gallacher and the rest, he was forced to take refuge in interviews with Rod and Emu and in the cornflake jungle of breakfast TV.

Peter Alliss on television (with Renton Laidlaw on radio not far behind) is, for me, by far the most knowledgeable, entertaining and tolerant sports commentator in the business: one who, incidentally, never makes a snide or jealous remark about football and cricket. Or even darts. But Peter's advent on the screen is not the only reason why Michael now feeds in other pastures. Far from not registering as a spectator sport, golf has become immensely popular, not only with golfers but with viewers and listeners of every age and condition. The crowds at the Open and the viewing and listening figures compiled by the BBC and ITV are proof of that.

As an elder of the Kirk I have a duty to pay regular visits to certain old ladies in the village. They never handled a golf club in their lives; but when 'the golf' is on television they are seated solidly in front of their sets, and I know that if I knocked on their doors at such times my welcome would be less than cordial. This suits me well, of course: without feeling guilty of dereliction of duty I can continue watching, too.

Yes, poor Michael. As an old caddy said to the South African tycoon, handicap 13, who surveyed the Old Course from the first tee at St Andrews and reckoned that it looked easy: 'Man, ye're haverin'!'

Then, according to Jock, we have said little about the future of golf. When you come to think about it, however, since a shepherd started whacking a pebble around a Scottish hillside with his upturned crook, the *idea* and *spirit* of the game have not changed at all and are unlikely to do so as long as it remains in existence. Alone with your Creator you are seeking perfection of swing and style; and in order to attain such perfection you are imposing salutary discipline on both mind and body, which as Euclid might have said, is the object of the exercise. In a way it resembles the game of life; and in life the essential principles do not change.

On the other hand, the appurtenances of golf are constantly changing: clubs, balls, clothing, the texture of greens, clubhouse rules and facilities.

Both King James IV and Mary Queen of Scots would be astonished by the sight – and sound – of metal 'woods' and multi-coloured golf balls. They would squirm in their royal robes when confronted by such as Brian Barnes or Nancy Lopez in their brief and colourful attire; and their squirming, I suspect, would be done in envy. They would look with envy also on the shorn beauty of a first-class modern course, comparing it with the unkempt roughness of the ground on which *they* had to putt and over which they had to drive, teeing up, according to legend, 'within one club's length of the hole'.

Being accustomed to palaces, they might not be so taken aback by the clubhouses, with their warm locker-rooms, showers and foot-baths, spacious bars and dining-halls, though the fact that in these same clubhouses lords and ladies, artists and artisans, along with men and women of trade and commerce all dine and drink together might cause them surprise. Not so much surprise as might be imagined, however. As far back as 1320, in the Arbroath Declaration, Robert the Bruce was reminded by his fellow Scots that as long as he led them in their fight for freedom they would give him full support but that if he displeased them they would immediately sack him and 'choose another King'. (Captains, secretaries, greens conveners, 'think on these things'.)

In golf, democracy is the name of the game. And so, while I believe that the idea and the spirit will remain constant, I believe also that change will inevitably take place in some of the material aspects. And why not? There is even something to be said for the new handicapping system, which judges us on our average performance and not on one or two rushes of blood to the head each season. And there may be something to be said also for maestro John Jacobs's new 'anti-slice' clubs, which Jock declares cause him to hook more powerfully than usual but which may spell joy for those of us struggling to overcome a slight fade. (At the same time, it is well to remember what Lee Trevino says: 'You can talk to a fade, but a hooked shot won't listen!') In the final issue, however, as has often occurred in the past, if any change threatens to undermine the ethics of golf, democracy will see to it that such a change is discarded.

Still reviewing the shortcomings of our round, I suggest we have been somewhat niggardly with practical advice. Jock points out that in spite of a hundred years of golfing experience between us we are not qualified – as is John Jacobs, for example – to act as teachers and that the serious instructional side of the game should be left to the professionals. All we can do – and we have tried to do it – is to present certain 'wise saws and modern instances' which we believe have been of help to us.

For example, I did not flinch from describing my attack of the Black Yips; and my left foot forward method of quelling, if not actually curing them reminds Jock of some advice once given by James Braid to his newly appointed assistant, Ross Whitehead. Braid took the young man out to a yawning cross-bunker at Walton Heath and made him take up a stance as if he were about to play a shot from the bunker's upward-sloping grass face. 'That,' said Braid, 'is the feeling you must always have at address.' Even when addressing the ball with a putter?

At this point Jock produces a quotation from *The Art of Golf* by Sir Walter Simpson, who was captain of the Honourable Company shortly before they moved from Musselburgh to Muirfield around 1892. He thinks I might well have used it in what he calls my 'horror story' concerning the yips.

Sir Walter wrote:

When a putter is waiting his turn to hole-out a putt of one or two feet in length, on which the match hangs at the last hole, it is of vital importance that he think of nothing. At this supreme moment he ought studiously to fill his mind with vacancy. He must not prepare himself to accept the gloomy face of his partner and the derisive delight of his adversaries with Christian resignation should he miss.

I agree that Sir Walter's advice is, indeed, profound. On the other hand I disagree with his negative approach and explain to Jock that it would have been inappropriate to use the quotation in a chapter designed to help in a positive way. My belief is that while you are putting the mind ought to be filled not with 'vacancy' but with happy thoughts: thoughts which 'drive out the killing care'. In any case, 'filled with vacancy' is a contradiction in terms, in much the same category of black humour as Gordon Peters's breathless remark after sinking a four-foot putt in a Walker Cup Match in America: 'I was trembling with bravery.'

We pour out two more drams of Old Machrimore.

Jock wonders why I have not written more fully about golf in old age, subtly implying that in this area at least I am an expert. 'Here at Dunaverty and Machrihanish,' he says, 'you are awash with OAPs, most of them with remarkably low handicaps. Sheriff Donald, for example, Boskers, Jim McPhee, Big Allan and Big Cecil, Johnny Burgoyne, Duncan Colville, John Trappe, Howard Wilson – '

' "Awash",' I interrupt him, 'is an ill-chosen word.' I take a disciplined sip from my refilled glass. 'Quite apart from the fact that the Mull of Kintyre is a notable health resort (especially for composers of pop songs), all those you mention are faithful golfers, and faithful golfers are inclined, barring accidents or suicide, to outlive their allotted span, simply because, in every sense, golf is a healthy game. It is also a game in which acquired skills and a national handicapping system enable you to compete on equal terms with your youngers and betters, even though your swing is more laboured – and more painful – than theirs.

'I hope you will remember that,' I tell my son. 'Remember, too, that when your drives become shorter and you find the holes becoming longer, at the same time you will find the fairways becoming wider.'

While he ponders this 'wise saw' and swallows another mouthful from his glass, I proceed quickly to emphasize that one of the glories of golf is that you can play it – and enjoy it – as long as you can walk.

I instance Sam Snead and John Panton, both OAPs but still loving their golf. I instance the late Bill Adwick, who at eighty-three, playing in the British Senior Professional Championship at Longniddry, returned a score of 78. Norman Mair of the *Sunday Standard* tells me that following this remarkable round he interviewed Bill's son, Ken Adwick, who competes with John Jacobs as the golf instructor *par excellence*. Ken said that though his father was 'long past beating balls on the practice ground for hours on end, he still subjected himself to an invaluable practice session whereby he simply sat down in an armchair, closed his eyes and thought about his swing, visualized it, rehearsed it'.

I instance, too, my old friend, the late Sammy Mitchell. Sammy was always of a sporting bent. As a young man, in 1912, he was one of the first to drive a panting, steaming car over the notorious Rest-and-be-Thankful hill in Argyll. At the age of fifty-five he took up golf with the same enthusiasm as he had once applied to motoring and, despite rheumatic pains, constant poisoning (as he chewed tobacco) and an irascible temperament, got his handicap down to 16 in less than a twelvemonth.

Shortly after World War II he and I were drawn together in the 'Amod-McNeil', Dunaverty's unofficial foursomes championship. In those years I could hit the ball a reasonable distance, while my partner's pitching and putting were tinged with genius. We won the handsome silver quaich, and Sammy's hoarse proclamations of triumph were frequently heard in the clubhouse.

A few years later, by chance, we were drawn together for a second time, and though by this time Sammy was bent almost double with rheumatism we won the quaich again.

During this second partnership I was amazed by his spirit. Most of his shots through the green were played with what he called a 'baffy', an ancient club, hickory-shafted, which resembled a modern 5-wood. Even when within thirty or forty yards of the putting surface he would order his caddy to produce his 'wee baffy' and then, almost invariably, lay the shot close to the flag. When putting, I was always conscious of him standing behind me, bloodshot eyes boring into my back, willing me to put the ball into the hole. Which I did, quite often, out of sheer terror, because Sammy's remarks about a feeble shot, uttered in a voice like that of a sergeant-major with croup, were always scathing. They were also liable to be accompanied by a long spittle of tobacco-juice directed at your shoes. Oddly enough, when he himself fluffed a shot and

an opponent tried to needle him about it he would retort with
some vigour: 'I'm entitled tae dae it! That's what my bloody
handicap's for!'

In the semi-final Sammy and I had to play the opposing
couple three times before ultimately beating them at the 53rd
hole. What happened on the 53rd green remains in my
memory like a gruesome Hogarth cartoon.

We were one up with two to play and one of our opponents
– who, in fact, was even older than Sammy – was faced with a
putt of 15 inches on the 17th green to save the match. I was
about to concede it when a low growl occurred behind me. I
turned. Sammy was there as usual. His expression was
fiendish. He was chewing his tobacco so fast that a brown
froth flecked his lips. His red-rimmed eyes were blazing. He
was moving his head from side to side with terrible emphasis.
I remained silent.

Our opponent bent to his putt. A squirt of tobacco-juice
flashed past my left leg and landed on the grass near the hole.
Nobody spoke, but I saw our opponent flinch. He resettled
himself. Then, after a long pause, he sighed as if surrendering
the spirit, yipped slightly and missed the putt. Sammy and I
were through.

As we walked down the 18th fairway towards the clubhouse
Sammy was staggering a little with physical pain and exhaustion. But he was chuckling, leering up into my face with
tobacco-stained glee. 'I kent he wad miss it!' he was saying. 'I
kent he wad miss it!'

He surveyed a patch of ground near the 18th green which
was raddled with daisies. Only a day or two before, when his
ball had been temporarily lost among them, he had been
cursing the greens convener and the greenkeeper with
outlandish violence. Now his attitude was different. 'Man,
Angus,' he said in a hoarse whisper, which he knew would
carry to our dejected opponents, trudging behind, 'man,
Angus, are they no' bonny, the wee daisies!'

Jock shakes his head as he supplies both of us with 'one
more for the road'. 'You and Sammy ought to have been
ashamed of yourselves, acting like children. I imagined that in

old age your approach to golf became increasingly calmer and more benign.'

Glass in hand, I decide to be a shade pompous. 'I saw a motto once, hanging above a man's desk. It went something like this: "Youth is not a time of life, it is a state of mind. You are as young as your faith, as old as your doubt; as young as your self-confidence, as old as your fear; as young as your hope, as old as your despair." '

Dusk is falling over the links of Dunaverty. In the clubhouse lights are going on. Jock suggests that to end the day I should tell the true story of the happy golfer from Oban. I point out that I have told it before, in a book.

'It was in all the newspapers as well.' He leans back comfortably. 'So never mind. It deserves a repeat.'

'All right, Jock. Here goes.' Old Machrimore is working well.

With eleven club-mates the happy golfer from Oban came to play a match against a local team at Machrihanish, over the hill from Dunaverty. After the golf a pleasant evening was enjoyed by everyone. Eventually, however, goodbyes had to be said, and at a late hour the Oban team climbed aboard their bus and began the long journey home.

Alas, in the excitement of departure a miscount had taken place. The happy golfer, unnoticed by his friends, was left behind, under a sofa.

Some time after midnight he woke up, alone in an empty clubhouse. At first he was upset. Then the natural resilience of a faithful golfer asserted itself. Clubs slung on his shoulder, he climbed out through a window and began to walk to Oban, a hundred miles to the north.

The night was dark, and before long he lost his way. Undaunted, he strode on, unaware that he was now entering the huge security complex of the NATO air base at Machrihanish. On all sides were eight-foot-high barbed-wire fences, snarling guard dogs and eagle-eyed police, but he remained oblivious of such formidable obstacles. The human and canine patrols remained oblivious of him.

Suddenly he saw in front a large vehicle. Exhausted after a long day, he probably thanked his lucky stars that against all the odds he had overtaken the Oban bus. He clambered in, found a seat near the back, deposited his clubs on the floor and settled down to sleep.

Hours later he opened his eyes. The bus was moving, but was it merely the state of his head that caused its engine to sound so rough?

In need of a cigarette, the happy golfer approached the driver and politely asked for a light. Equally polite, the driver handed over his lighter with the remark: 'May I ask who you are, sir?'

The happy golfer was caught unprepared. 'One of the Oban golfers,' he said. 'Isn't this the bus?'

For the pilot and crew of the Hercules aircraft bound for a secret destination in England, the moment was traumatic. Entering the plane, ready for take-off, they had seen the happy golfer asleep at the back, his clubs beside him. Imagining he must be a VIP with official clearance, on his way to play golf with friends in the south, they had decided not to disturb him. Now they knew better. Were they face to face with a hi-jacker, or even an international spy?

The great plane banked round, teetering on one wing. As it roared back to Machrihanish radio signals buzzed and crackled in the air.

The Hercules landed. The happy golfer's dream was over. Bothered and bewildered, the sound of sharp questions and police sirens echoing in his ears, he was arrested, dragged down the gangway steps, thrust into a Black Maria and, later, clapped into gaol in Campbeltown.

In the outcome, of course, he was released. Nothing at all happened to him. The whole thing was what Sir Robin Day might have described on radio or television as 'an almighty cock-up'.

But I salute the happy golfer. He proved once again that even in these days of cold business endeavour and callous bureaucracy, camouflaged by mind-bending propaganda, not all the King's horses nor all the King's men can defeat the innocent human spirit.

Which, I believe, is the spirit of golf.

Index